95
0

THE CHRISTIAN WORSHIPING

THE

CHRISTIAN

WORSHIPING

V. L. Stanfield

Convention Press

NASHVILLE   TENNESSEE

Code Number: Church Study Course
This book is number 0612 in category 6,
section for Adults and Young People

Library of Congress Catalog Card Number: 65–10324
Printed in the United States of America
85. s 64 R.R.D

Contents

About the Author

VERNON LATRELLE STANFIELD is a native of Atlanta, Missouri. He received his A.B. degree from Northeast Missouri State Teachers College. He has done additional study at Northwestern University, Columbia University, Union Theological Seminary, and Oxford University.

Dr. Stanfield received his Th.M. and Th.D. degrees from Southern Baptist Theological Seminary, Louisville, Kentucky. He served on the faculty of the Southern Seminary from 1946–59 as assistant, associate, and professor of preaching. He has been the pastor of churches in Missouri and Indiana and interim pastor of many churches.

After he left Southern Baptist Theological Seminary in 1959, Dr. Stanfield became professor of preaching at the New Orleans Baptist Theological Seminary.

Dr. Stanfield, a writer as well as a popular speaker, is author of *The Favorite Sermons of John A. Broadus,* published in 1959, and is a contributor to *The Encyclopedia of Southern Baptists.* His articles, dealing mainly with preaching and Christian worship, appear frequently in theological journals and Baptist periodicals.

Church Study Course

THE CHURCH STUDY COURSE began October 1, 1959. It is a merger of three courses previously promoted by the Sunday School Board —the Sunday School Training Course, the Graded Training Union Study Course, and the Church Music Training Course. On October 1, 1961, the Woman's Missionary Union principles and methods studies were added.

The course is fully graded. The system of awards provides a series of five diplomas of twenty books each for Adults or Young People, two diplomas of five books each for Intermediates, and two diplomas of five books each for Juniors.

The course is comprehensive, with books grouped into twenty categories. The purpose of the course is to help Christians to grow in knowledge and conviction, to help them to grow toward maturity in Christian character and competence for service, to encourage them to participate worthily as workers in their churches, and to develop leaders for all phases of church life and work.

The Church Study Course is promoted by the Baptist Sunday School Board, 127 Ninth Avenue, North, Nashville, Tennessee, through its Sunday School, Training Union, Church Music, and Church Administration departments; and the Woman's Missionary Union, 600 North Twentieth Street, Birmingham, Alabama; and by the respective departments in the states affiliated with the Southern Baptist Convention. A description of the course and the system of awards may be found in the leaflet "Trained Workmen," which may be obtained without charge from any one of these departments named.

A record of all awards earned should be maintained in each church. A person should be designated by the church to keep the files. Forms for such records may be ordered from any Baptist Book Store.

Requirements for Credit in Class or Home Study

IF CREDIT IS DESIRED for the study of this book in a class or by home study, the following requirements must be met:

I. IN CLASSWORK

1. The class must meet a minimum of seven and one-half clock hours. The required time does not include assembly periods. Ten class periods of forty-five minutes each are recommended. (If laboratory or clinical work is desired in specialized or technical courses, this requirement may be met by six clock hours of classwork and three clock hours of supervised laboratory or clinical work.)

2. A class member who attends all class sessions and completes the reading of the book within a week following the last class session will not be required to do any written work.

3. A class member who is absent from one or more sessions must answer the questions on all chapters he misses. In such a case, he must turn in his paper within a week, and he must certify that he has read the book.

4. The teacher should request an award for himself. A person who teaches a book in the section for Intermediates or Juniors of any category or conducts an approved unit of instruction for Nursery, Beginner, or Primary children will be granted an award in category 11, Special Studies, which will count as an elective on his own diploma. He should specify in his request the name of the book taught, or the unit conducted for Nursery, Beginner, or Primary children.

5. The teacher should complete the "Request for Book Awards —Class Study" (Form 150) and forward it within two weeks after the completion of the class to the Church Study Course Awards Office, 127 Ninth Avenue, North, Nashville, Tennessee 37203.

II. IN HOME STUDY

1. A person who does not attend any class session may receive credit by answering all questions for written work as indicated in the book. When a person turns in his paper on home study, he must certify that he has read the book.

2. Students may find profit in studying the text together, but individual papers are required. Carbon copies or duplicates in any form cannot be accepted.

3. Home study work papers may be graded by the pastor or a person designated by him, or they may be sent to the Church Study Course Awards Office for grading. The form entitled "Request for Book Awards—Home Study" (Form 151) must be used in requesting awards. It should be mailed to Church Study Course Awards Office, 127 Ninth Avenue, North, Nashville, Tennessee 37203.

III. CREDIT FOR THIS BOOK

This book is number 0612 in category 6, section for Adults and Young People.

CHAPTER 1 OUTLINE

I. REASONS FOR THE IMPORTANCE OF WORSHIP
   1. To Sustain a Sense of Oneness with God
   2. To Fulfil Our Need for Fellowship
   3. To Give Purpose and Meaning to Life
   4. To Make Us Aware of Our Limitations
   5. To Find Answers to Life's Problems
   6. To Gain Strength to Live Abundantly
   7. To Change Perspective
   8. To Receive Instruction
   9. To Renew a Desire for Service
   10. To Receive Salvation and Assurance

II. EXAMPLES OF THE UNDERVALUATION OF WORSHIP
   1. In the Christian World
   2. In Southern Baptist Churches
   3. By Southern Baptist Seminaries
   4. By Many Pastors
   5. By Individual Christians

III. A DEVELOPING APPRECIATION OF WORSHIP
   1. In Southern Baptist Literature
   2. In Southern Baptist Seminaries
   3. In Southern Baptist Churches

1

The Importance of Worship

"BELIEVE ME, the most effective thing that the church of Christ can do in the world, and the most effective thing that any individual Christian can do, is to lift up his heart in the adoration of God." So declared the late Archbishop William Temple.[1]

To worship God—to adore him, to commune with him, to offer self to him—is the highest expression of the Christian's relationship with his God. Christians believe the worship of God is important and necessary. The evangelical Christian may want to point out that there is no conflict between his worship and his witness. Because he knows God in Christ and worships him, his obligation to witness to others is important. Christians agree, however, that worship is important for the life of the church. Chapter 8 discusses worship and witness more at length.

I. REASONS FOR THE IMPORTANCE OF WORSHIP

Many Christians take part regularly in both private and public worship. They insist that their worship is meaningful and helpful. They declare that this worship is indispensable to their Christian life, and they are quick to offer reasons for this.

1. *To Sustain a Sense of Oneness with God*

Worship helps man to sustain a oneness with God. Man is a creature made in the image of God. He has an innate desire to be with God. Yet his freedom to choose and to act leads him to wrong choices and wrong actions. In spite of highest resolutions, his sin stands between him and God. Paul's experience is common to man, "For the good that I would I do not: but the evil which I would not, that I do" (Rom. 7:19). When man is separated from God, he is not happy. His rebellion brings misery, rather than peace. There is a hunger to be at one with God.

Here is where worship helps. As man worships, he confronts a holy God. In the presence of a righteous God, he sees his own sin. He is suddenly aware that his disobedience has separated him from God. Since he does not want to stay away from God, he is led to confess his sin. Because the righteous God is a forgiving God, man is reconciled with God and finds peace. In contrition and humility, man dedicates himself anew to God and finds peace.

Because man drifts and God seeks him, man needs to worship. In worship, he is restored to the only place where he is completely happy—as a child of God at one with his Father.

2. To Fulfil Our Need for Fellowship

Worship fulfils the needs for fellowship with others. Just as a man hungers for fellowship with God, he also desires fellowship with others. Man is a social being. After he created man, God saw that it was "not good for man to be alone." Man instinctively feels that he should not be alone. He shuns isolation. He wants to belong, to be a part of a group.

This sense of belonging has its greatest fulfilment in the worship by the church. Men meet together, they greet each other, and they join together in praise and prayer. Men share in testimony, they listen to the preacher's exhortation, and they ask the blessing of God upon each other. Thus they truly belong. They are partakers one with the other. They are really together—of one mind, one heart, and one spirit. In this way, man's fellowship is wonderfully fulfilled.

3. To Give Purpose and Meaning to Life

Worship gives meaning and purpose to life. To understand life and to know its meaning is a deep hunger within every man. Many questions arise within him and cry out for answers: Who am I? What am I? From whence did I come? Where am I going? What is my destiny, and who shapes it?

As man worships God, the light of divine truth floods his soul. He is a creation of God. He is a child of God. God gave him the breath of life. He now understands his origin. Moreover, God, who created man, provided for his redemption. He did not spare his own Son, but gave him to save all men. As each man trusts Christ, he experiences the joy of salvation and the reality of everlasting life.

Now man knows his origin and destiny—the purpose of his life. He is a child of God. He is to serve God. One day, he will dwell with God. This gives to life a new dimension, a new importance, and a new sense of worth. Man feels truly that his chief end is to glorify God and to enjoy him forever.

4. To Make Us Aware of Our Limitations

Worship makes man aware of his limitations. When man communes with the infinite, almighty, and eternal God, he realizes anew how limited, weak, and temporary he is. In the presence of the Creator, man is aware of his creatureliness.

Man easily forgets the brevity of his life and the fleeting nature of his existence. He often develops a spirit of independence and self-sufficiency. He then tries to live by bread alone. However, he is not happy, and he is not at peace within himself. He may not know the reason for this dissatisfaction. But when he worships, he knows that his life has not been whole.

In the presence of God, he rediscovers his creatureliness. He cannot be independent of his God. In God, he lives and moves and has his being. In and through God, the earthly becomes eternal, and the corruptible becomes incorruptible. In the presence of the infinite God, man sees himself as he is and turns again to the one who can make his life complete.

5. *To Find the Answers to Life's Problems*

The worshiper finds answers to life's problems. Life has many problems; and few people, if any, escape them. Tension, illness, disappointments, frustration, sorrow, and sinfulness are common to the life of man.

Jesus' invitation to worship promises help: "Come unto me, all ye that labour and are heavy laden, and I will give you rest" (Matt. 11:28). The man who falls prostrate before God in sincere worship will find rest unto his soul.

God is a God of comfort. The term "to comfort" means "to strengthen." God, who is a God of love and mercy, delights in healing man's infirmities, sharing his burdens, and forgiving his sin. Many persons have entered a service with heavy, grievous burdens and have left with joy in their hearts and a song on their lips. The miracle of worship has taken place; burdens shared with God have been lifted. The truth of the Word of God has been fulfilled: "They that wait upon the Lord shall renew their strength; they shall mount up with wings as eagles; they shall run, and not be weary; and they shall walk, and not faint" (Isa. 40:31).

6. *To Gain Strength to Live Abundantly*

In worship, there is strength to live abundantly. Quite apart from the problems of life, every man needs strength to live the good life. In his best moments, each man wants his life to be full, rich, and complete. This was God's longing for man before it was man's wish for himself. Jesus declared, "I am come that they might have life, and that they might have it more abundantly" (John 10:10).

In the act of worship, this high desire finds its complete

fulfilment; for in this worship, man recognizes his littleness and his inadequacy. He opens his life to the unlimited resources of his God. Through the ministry of the Holy Spirit, he is given new power, new strength, new insight, and new wisdom. For a time at least, he is much more than he was. With God's resources undergirding and infilling him, he can fulfil his resolutions and live on a higher plane. Only in worship can man find the secret of abundant living. Man by himself can never achieve wholeness, but man plus God equals the full, rich, complete, and abundant life as God intended it.

7. To Change Perspective

Worship gives a new perspective. When man follows only his own directions, he gets mixed up. He begins to look *in* rather than *out*. His life becomes cluttered with things, and he misdirects his energies. Then "worship comes as a gracious corrective." [2]

Through his worship, man is led out of himself. When brought into intimate communion with God, he forgets himself and begins to think of others. His inner motivation is changed, and with this change there is healing.

As man worships, his attention is turned from the material to the spiritual. Physical things lose their attraction. While things are a necessary part of life, they must be kept in proper relationship. They must be kept as a means to an end, as helps along the way, and never as ends in themselves. By worship, man is directed again to "seek ye first the kingdom of God, and his righteousness" (Matt. 6:33).

By worship, man is led to redirect his energies. He often gets caught in the treadmill of life and gives his best strength to the trivial and the unimportant. But, as the result of his communion with God, man sees again that he should love God with all of his mind, heart, soul, and strength, and his neighbor as himself.

8. *To Receive Instruction*

In worship, man receives instruction. He is taught; he is strengthened. This instruction comes from different sources.

As the pastor or some other worshiper reads the Scriptures, God, through his Holy Spirit, speaks to the mind and heart of the worshiper. There is new spiritual light, new guidance, and new teaching.

Then the pastor seeks to expound a Bible passage. He explains its meaning, he illustrates it, and he applies it to life. The one who was promised to bring all things to our remembrance, the Holy Spirit, then works in the heart to instruct.

Hymns and prayers offer instruction, too. A person may have sung a hymn many times, but in a particular hour of worship some stanza has new meaning. It provides new spiritual instruction. As the worship leader offers a prayer with the group, some new relationship to God is sensed by those sharing the prayer.

God has invited man not only to believe, but to know. In the miracle of worship, mentally accepted facts become experienced facts. To be instructed by the Holy Spirit is to know.

9. *To Renew a Desire for Service*

Worship renews a desire to serve God. Worship and service are interchangeable terms, and they should be inseparable. "Worship ought to drive us to action, action once more to worship. . . . To try either to serve God without worshiping or to worship without service is to debase and enfeeble both pursuits." [3]

In worship, man hears the command of God to do his work. The worshiper catches a vision of the work to be done. But with the vision of the work comes the desire and the energy to do it. As man wearies in service, he returns to his source of help. Many churchgoers have seen this motto on a bulletin board or in a bulletin: "Enter to worship—Depart to serve." Only through worship can this essential motto become an actual reality.

10. *To Receive Salvation and Assurance*

Perhaps the most important reason for worship is that as man turns to God he receives the gift of salvation. As he continues to worship, the child of God knows the assurance of his sonship.

Since the first man disobeyed and sinned and became estranged from God, God has taken the initiative in redemption. God's last and mighty act of redemption was to give his Son, Jesus Christ. "While we were yet sinners, Christ died for us" (Rom. 5:8).

When man seeks God, who has already sought him, man meets God. As man repents of his sin and invites Christ into his heart, he receives the gift of salvation. "As many as received him, to them gave he power to become the sons of God" (John 1:12). As the child of God communes with his Heavenly Father, he has the assurance of his sonship to the Father.

For ye have not received the spirit of bondage again to fear; but ye have received the spirit of adoption. . . . The Spirit . . . beareth witness with our spirit, that we are the children of God (Rom. 8:15–16).

These are ten reasons why worship is important. When these reasons are carefully weighed, they explain why worship should be magnified rather than undervalued. Consider now some examples of the undervaluation of worship.

II. EXAMPLES OF THE UNDERVALUATION OF WORSHIP

In spite of the high claims for the place of worship in the life of the Christian and of the church, these claims do not seem to be translated into worship. In fact, there seems to be both a conscious and an unconscious depreciation of worship. The value of worship to the Christian has been lowered. One does not have to delve deeply into worship practices today to discover this. He may discover it on any given Sunday in his own church.

1. *In the Christian World*

Throughout the Christian world, high ideals of worship do not appear to be taken seriously.

The lack of participation in both public and private worship proves this. Some church members never engage in corporate, or public, worship; others worship only a few times a year. It is estimated that only 50 per cent of those on church membership rolls share in public worship. In Great Britain, less than 10 per cent of the people participate in public worship. In the United States, a so-called Christian land, only about 20 per cent of the people engage in public worship on any particular Sunday. Moreover, the number of church people who engage in regular, planned private worship would be even smaller than the number who share in public worship.

Many Christians have little understanding of the nature of worship. They know little about the meaning and purpose of the term "worship." Even Christians with books about worship have not bothered to examine the history or content of these books. The average Christian could not give a concise, usable definition of Christian worship. Consequently, many worshipers could not answer yes to the question, "Understandest thou what thou doest?" A study of this book can help them to understand this vital function.

2. *In Southern Baptists Churches*

The undervaluation of worship found in much of the Christian world is also true of Southern Baptists. Some Southern

Baptist churches hold worship services more often than other Christian churches do. However, many Southern Baptists neither share regularly in public worship nor, so far as is known, engage in private worship.

There is evidence that many Southern Baptists do not even understand the nature of worship. Many church people tend to think of a preaching service, not a worship service. They often say, "Let's go to preaching," rather than, "Let us go to worship God." A church member may enter a service fifteen minutes late and say to himself, "I have not missed anything. The preacher has not started." Preaching is worship; but so are the singing of hymns, praying, Scripture reading, and giving an offering. The worship service has many parts, and all are important. Southern Baptists may have this view of worship because, too often, they have been invited to "come and hear the sermon" or to "come to preaching," rather than to "come and worship with us."

Southern Baptists also tend to undervalue worship by misdirecting it. Worship directed to anyone but the Lord God is not true worship. Often, services that are "preacher-centered" are man-centered, not God-centered. This ultimately leads to idol worship. To be sure, this transferal of worship from God to man is unconscious; but it is real. The deacon's familiar prayer for the preacher, "Hide him behind the cross!" should be realized more often. To direct worship to anyone or anything but God is to undervalue it. It is misdirected worship.

3. By Southern Baptist Seminaries

It would be assumed that the undervaluation of worship found in the Christian world and among Southern Baptists would not be found in Southern Baptist seminaries. Yet, worship is underrated even in our schools. Future pastors are given the finest theoretical and practical training, but the practical training does not always include a course in the theory and practice of worship. Often, this training comes from the pastorate.

Currently, only one Southern Baptist seminary specifically requires its ministerial students to take a course in worship. Elective courses are offered, but only a minority of students elect to take them. How can pastors effectively lead in worship when they have not been trained in such leadership? How can pastors plan attractive, meaningful worship services when they have not been instructed in the principles of worship planning?

Seminary students carry with them the pattern of participation found in their churches. Unless there is a "big-name" speaker, only 25 to 50 per cent of the community shares in the regular worship service. Some do not even have regular Sunday worship as a part of their schedule. All of this indicates that the worship of God is not primary in the training or thinking of future pastors.

4. By Many Pastors

Some pastors give little attention to Christian worship and to worship leadership. Many pastors do not think of themselves as leaders of worship. In seminary classes and in pastors' conferences, this question was asked of preachers: What are the duties which you perform? The answers, when compiled, made a long list. Rarely did a pastor say, "I am a leader of worship." The pastor who has never thought of himself as a worship leader is not likely to magnify worship.

The pastor who does not think of himself as a leader of worship usually gives little time to planning the worship service. A pastor may spend eight, ten, or even twenty hours preparing a twenty-five-minute sermon. Yet, he may give no time to the public prayers, which may take eight minutes of the service. He may spend only a few minutes helping to select the hymns, which will take ten to twelve minutes of the service time. If time generally is given to that which is rated high, then it follows that the total worship service is often rated low.

A pastor may talk about "preaching and worship," rather than "preaching in worship." This announcement was made once: "We will not have a sermon; we will have a worship service." There should be no such separation. Preaching is worship. Ideally, God speaks through the preacher. Can there be any higher act of worship than this? When the sermon is not understood to be worship, worship is undervalued.

5. By Individual Christians

Many individual Christians place little value on worship. They rarely take part in worship services. When questioned about their failure to share in worship, they answer like this: "Worship does nothing for me." "It leaves me cold!" Said one teen-ager, "The hour in church is such a waste!"

Others would have to confess concerning private worship: "I never read the Bible. I never pray. I just do not take the time." Individual Christians often show no interest in worship.

III. A Developing Appreciation of Worship

There are signs on the horizon that interest in Christian worship is at a new high. In many denominations, there is growing interest in studies on worship. An intensive interest in every facet of worship is developing. Some of that interest is beginning to appear in Southern Baptist churches and to be shown by some Southern Baptist pastors.

1. In Southern Baptist Literature

For years, the Sunday School and Training Union Departments have stressed the importance of worship in the unit organizations of a church. They have implemented this by suggesting materials and orders of service. Recent Church Study Course materials have emphasized worship in the life of the Christian and the church. Worship has been seen as one of the major functions of a church. The whole area of church functions is being investigated for the churches and denomination.

2. *In Southern Baptist Seminaries*

In recent years, elective classes in Christian worship have been offered in most Southern Baptist seminaries. These elective classes in Christian worship have had an increasing appeal to students. One seminary has required courses. Perhaps the time is near when every seminary graduate will have required training in worship and worship leadership.

3. *In Southern Baptist Churches*

In Southern Baptist churches, there is a growing dissatisfaction with the ill-planned worship that calls little attention to God. The people want to meet God. Pastors are striving to plan services in which God and his people may meet. To worship God in truth and in spirit is a growing desire in the hearts of many people.

NOTES

[1] *Basic Convictions* (New York: Harper & Bros., 1936), p. 19.

[2] Clarice Bowman, *Restoring Worship* (New York: Abingdon-Cokesbury Press, 1951), p. 21.

[3] Georgia Harkness, *Prayer and the Common Life* (New York: Abingdon Press, 1948), p. 150.

QUESTIONS TO STIMULATE DISCUSSION

1. How many Christians live in your town or city? How many share in worship each Sunday? How many members are in your church? How many worship each Lord's Day?

2. Do you engage in regular private worship?

3. What happens when people become displeased with the pastor? Do they cease to worship God?

4. How has engaging in private and public worship helped you? Is your interest in worship growing or declining? Give reasons for your answer.

CHAPTER 2 OUTLINE

I. A SEARCH FOR DEFINITION
1. Etymological
2. Biblical
3. Contemporary
4. Personal

II. SOME CHARACTERISTICS OF CHRISTIAN WORSHIP
1. Centered in God
2. Personal
3. Corporate
4. Sincere
5. Humble
6. Spiritual
7. Free and Spontaneous
8. Expressed in Life

2

The Nature of Worship

SINCE WORSHIP IS SO IMPORTANT in the life of the Christian and in the life of the church, its nature must be understood. The definitions of worship are many, and the number and variety of these definitions are increasing. Yet to find a completely satisfying definition of worship is not easy. Even though church members participate and ministers lead in worship, many have never tried to define it.

There may be a good reason for not describing the experience of worship. It is a spiritual experience; it is entering into spiritual communion with the Lord Most High. Such a relationship cannot be imprisoned in a verbal formula. It defies definition. Nonetheless, worship will be more meaningful if the worshiper has some understanding of its nature.

I. A SEARCH FOR DEFINITION

What does worship really mean? To worship is to do what? Where may insight into the nature of worship be found? Several areas offer help. Perhaps the place to begin is with the word "worship."

1. *Etymological*

A study of the etymology, or origin, of the word "worship" will help one understand its nature.

The word "worship" is of Anglo-Saxon beginning. It was originally spelled *worthship* or *weorthscipe,* and it was a combination of two words: "worth" and "ship." In usage, it came to be the word "worship" and meant ascribing worth to a person or thing of value. An important government or church personage once was addressed as "Your Worship."

Christian worship is the ascription of supreme worth to God. He is the one, and the only one, worthy of worship. He is God; he is the Supreme Worth; he is worthy of the greatest recognition. The psalmist with true insight declared: "For the Lord is a great God, and a great King above all gods. In his hand are the deep places of the earth: the strength of the hills is his also. The sea is his, and he made it: and his hands formed the dry land. O come, let us worship and bow down: let us kneel before the Lord our maker" (Psalm 95:3-6).

2. *Biblical*

A study of the Bible will also give added insight into the nature of worship. Several words in the Bible are translated "worship," but a look at one Hebrew word and one Greek word will be helpful.

The Hebrew word most frequently translated "worship" is *shahah*. The word means "to bow down," "to depress oneself," "to prostrate oneself." In the Old Testament, the worshiper prostrated himself before Jehovah. *Shahah* expresses a reverential attitude of mind and body. The worshiper is in complete submission before God. This submission is God initiated: God is acting in the heart of the worshiper. This reverence has nothing to do with the edification of the worshiper. It is the person's recognition that God is God, and that he is worthy of all worship.

A Greek word frequently translated "worship" is *proskuneo*, which literally means "to kiss towards" or "to kiss the hand." Again, the picture is one of reverential awe, of bowing prostrate upon the ground in complete submission before God. This act also recognized God's worth. It is the worshiper's deliberate acceptance of a lowly place in the presence of a mighty God. Martin Luther exclaimed, "To have a God is to worship him."

In the New Testament, worship is also thought of as service. In fact, worship and service are inseparably united. In response to what God has done for him in Christ, man surrenders himself completely to God. After Paul had proclaimed that Christ offered redemption to all who believed in him, he said, "I appeal to you therefore, brethren, by the mercies of God, to present your bodies as a living sacrifice, holy and acceptable to God, which is your spiritual worship" (Rom. 12:1, RSV). Worship is the Christian's response of self-giving to God for what he has done in Christ.

In the biblical sense, man worships God because he is God and he is worthy of all worship. When man learns that salvation is his through Christ, when through faith he receives this salvation—then, in gratitude man offers himself to God.

3. Contemporary

More understanding of the nature of worship may be found in current definitions. In recent years, many definitions of worship have been given. As a result of the current interest in worship, new definitions are being added.

In his book *Reality in Worship,* Willard Sperry gave this definition: "Worship is the adoration of God, the ascription of supreme worth to God, and the manifestation of reverence in the presence of God." [1]

In his chapter "What Is Christian Worship?" Henry Sloane Coffin points out focal points of worship: "Worship is appreciation"; "Worship is offering"; and worship "is communion of God with men." [2]

A classic definition comes from the pen of William Temple. "To worship is to quicken the conscience by the holiness of God, to feed the mind with the truth of God, to purge the imagination by the beauty of God, to open the heart to the love of God, to devote the will to the purpose of God." [3]

A current concept of worship is given by Wilhelm Hahn:

Worship is God speaking to us and our response. "Worship is a twofold event: . . . God acts toward us, and we answer Him through what we do." [4] Hahn points out that the initiative lies with God. "Worship is first and foremost God's service to us. . . . Our activity in worship can be nothing more than reaction and response." [5]

These definitions have several things in common. First is the recognition and appreciation of God. True worship ascribes worth to God. Then follows communion, or fellowship, with God. Christian worship is a personal relationship between God who loves man and man who loves God. After appreciation and communion comes offering. As man bows down before God, he offers himself and all he is to God. All of this is done in a sense of awe and reverence—the creature is before his creator; finite man is before the Infinite God; sinful man is in the presence of a Holy God.

4. Personal

Any Christian who thinks seriously about worship arrives at some definition of it from his experience. Here is the writer's definition of worship: Worship is giving one's adoration, his praise, his money, himself to God, and then receiving the things which God gives those who freely turn to him.

Man does not worship God in order to receive. He does not drive a bargain with God. He offers himself to God and thus he receives from God. Here is observed a great Christian paradox: As man loses himself in the worship of God, he finds himself.

Too many worshipers leave a service saying, "I did not get anything; I was not helped." The reason for this failure is obvious. The worshiper has been trying to use God. It is at the heart of worship that man does not attempt to use God for his own purposes, but that he offers himself to God to be used for God's purposes. Each worshiper should analyze his experiences. He should ask, What does worship mean to me?

II. Some Characteristics of Christian Worship

A study of the characteristics of Christian worship also may increase one's understanding of the nature of worship.

1. *Centered in God*

The first and central characteristic of worship is that it is centered in God. Isaiah set the pattern for all true worship when he said, "I saw also the Lord sitting upon a throne, high and lifted up" (Isa. 6:1). God is enthroned; he is the Most High God.

In the Old Testament, God reveals himself as the God of majesty and power, the God of holiness, and the God of justice and mercy. But many more attributes of God are revealed in the New Testament. For God is revealed in Jesus Christ. John declared, "The Word was made flesh, and dwelt among us" (John 1:14). Jesus himself boldly claimed, "I and my Father are one" (John 10:30).

Philip wistfully requested, "Master, ... show us the Father: that is all we need."

"Have I been so long among you," Jesus answered, "and yet you, Philip, do not know me? He who has seen me has seen the Father" (John 14:8-9, Weymouth).

Paul insisted that God "has shone in our hearts to give the light of the knowledge of the glory of God in the face of Jesus Christ" (2 Cor. 4:6, Weymouth).

The New Testament explains how, when we know Christ, we know what God is like. For that which we see revealed in Christ, we may know to be the Father. Christ was love, purity, concern, kindness. Christ voluntarily gave himself in forgiving love. Now, men know God the Father and have access to him through Christ.

Man's understanding of God increased after the death, resurrection, and ascension of Jesus. Then came the Holy Spirit. God was present with men in the person and power of his Spirit. "Without any attempt at fine theological distinctions the New Testament writers speak of the omnipresence of God, the living presence of the resurrected Christ, and the continuous fellowship of the Holy Spirit as one and the same thing." [6]

Christian worship centers in the Lord God, fully revealed in Jesus Christ and fully present in the Holy Spirit. Today, true worship is not essentially a building, a form, or a leader. True worship centers in a great triune God.

2. Personal

Christian worship is personal. It is an intimate relationship between God and man. But God is not a vague, impersonal diety aloof from man. God is personal. He wants fellowship with man. In his Son, he dwelt among men. In his Spirit, he is available to men.

When Jesus taught his disciples to pray, he taught them to begin by saying, "Our Father." Here is a direct, personal encounter. As a child approaches his earthly father, so the child of God may approach his Heavenly Father. The worshiper speaks to God and knows that he listens; God speaks and man listens.

This relationship is expressed by the song "In the Garden":

> And He walks with me, and He talks with me,
>   And He tells me I am His own;
> And the joy we share as we tarry there,
>   None other has ever known.
>   —C. AUSTIN MILES

But this does not mean that the experience is subjective or that the worshiper has simply imagined the presence of God. Just as God took the initiative in man's salvation, he takes the initiative in every other experience of man. The experience of God's presence in worship is a spiritual miracle, but it is a miracle that comes about by the operation of the Holy Spirit. Through the Spirit, each worshiper has a personal encounter with God.

To say that worship is personal is not to deny its corporate nature. Worship is also corporate. This is worship by the group or congregation. However, each believer has his moment with God. This is certainly true of private worship, but even in larger groups each person is alone with God. Moreover, this vital, personal encounter is necessary in all Christian worship.

3. Corporate

Christian worship is not only personal, but it is also corporate, or group experienced. Personal worship is inherently corporate, because Christian worship cannot be offered without forgiveness in Christ and without union with Christ in his body. "So we, being many, are one body in Christ, and every one members one of another" (Rom. 12:5). To be "in Christ" is to be in the body of Christ. In baptism, the believer is symbolically united with Christ and with other believers. "For as the body is one, and hath many members, and all the members of that one body, being many, are one body: so also is Christ. For by one Spirit are we all baptized into one body" (1 Cor. 12:12-13).

The believer is received into something larger and more important than himself; he is a part of a living fellowship, the church. As church members worship together, the believer reaches his highest level of aspiration and inspiration.

Though private worship is valid and necesary, public worship is even more essential. It is not in isolation, but in fellowship that the worshiper knows a sense of oneness with God and with others. The Spirit comes to a waiting fellowship to instruct and empower.

Personal worship and corporate worship are not contradictory; they are complementary. The person's experience with God is verified and completed as it expresses the grace and love of God in service to others.

4. Sincere

Another characteristic of Christian worship is sincerity. Christian worship should be absolutely sincere. Morgan Phelps Noyes declares that sincerity is the first essential of true worship.[7]

Occasionally, acts of worship are fulfilled for the eyes and ears of men. A prayer may be said, not with the thought that God is listening, but that men are hearing. An anthem or a hymn may be sung, not to please God, but to gain the praise of men. Sometimes even the sermon is preached with the primary desire that it will be acceptable to men. Such acts of worship are not authentic or sincere and, according to the teaching of Jesus, have their own reward.

Worshipers and leaders of worship sometimes go through acts of worship casually and nonchalantly. The worship is performed perfunctorily. It lacks the ring of reality. God is not purposely left out; he is just unconsciously omitted. There is no clear intention to offer worship to God. It is easy for the less formal worshiper to feel that this kind of thing happens because a form is used, and that familiarity with form breeds contempt. However, sincerity is a quality of spirit, not the property of any particular method of worship. A minister may read a prayer nonchalantly or with great sincerity. Another minister may pray freely with complete sincerity, or he may pray without thinking. Regardless of the form, sincerity is indispensable for true worship.

5. Humble

Christian worshipers should also be humble. No worshiper should go before God full of pride and self-righteousness, reciting his own virtues. If he does, like the Pharisee he will leave the temple unjustified. Each worshiper should go before God as did the publican, confessing his sin and asking for mercy. The Scripture "Whosoever shall exalt himself shall be abased; and he that shall humble himself shall be exalted" (Matt. 23:12) is never more true than in worship.

Actually, genuine worship generates humility as few experiences can. For in worship, man not only sees himself as he really is, but he also sees himself as God sees him. Furthermore, he sees a Holy God. "No honest man can contemplate the holiness of God without a fresh and vivid awareness of his own unholiness." [8] As man sees his own sinfulness, he is brought low. He is humbled. Even as a worshiper bows his head in the presence of God, he expresses his humility. But as man bows before God, he places himself in the stream of God's mercy. And the God of mercy has a way of uplifting those who bow before him.

6. *Spiritual*

Christian worship is spiritual. Here the term "spiritual" is used with two different meanings. In one sense, it is the meaning of spirit with Spirit. "God is spirit, and those who worship him must worship in spirit and in truth" (John 4:24, RSV). The experience of true worship is an inward experience of heart and mind. Man turns from the external and material to the eternal and spiritual. Man's soul meets the one who gave to man the breath of life. Man is no longer conformed to the world, but he is transformed by the renewing of his mind.

Spiritual is also used to describe the activity of the Holy Spirit in the heart of the worshiper. The Holy Spirit was promised to the worshiper. "I will pray the Father, and he will give you another Counselor, to be with you for ever, even the Spirit of truth, whom the world cannot receive, because it neither sees him nor knows him; you know him, for he dwells with you, and will be in you" (John 14:16-17, RSV). This promise has been completely fulfilled.

The Holy Spirit is active in worship, or it is not true worship. The Holy Spirit takes the Word and instructs the mind. "He shall teach you all things" (John 14:26). The Holy Spirit uses all parts of the service to bring to remembrance the things of the Lord. It is he who quickens to salvation. It is he who restores the soul. He comforts and strengthens; he brings new dedication; he creates a sense of oneness. In other words, the Holy Spirit makes our worship effectual. True worship is spiritual.

7. Free and Spontaneous

Christian worship should be free and spontaneous. By free is meant the absence of absolutely fixed form. This is not to say that a particular service will not be well planned. Nor is it to say that the service will not be performed decently and in order. It is to say that the service may be changed and varied, that even the spontaneous and unexpected may take place.

In the New Testament, worship was Spirit filled and Spirit directed. The spontaneous and the unusual often occurred. The Spirit was present, and men responded to his guidance. Sometimes this led to emotional outbursts, such as "speaking in tongues" (1 Cor. 14), which sometimes needed to be curbed. But it also gave an unusual heart quality to the worship.

New Testament worshipers knew nothing of fixed orders or an unvariable order of worship. To be sure, certain elements were common to the services. Some examples are praise, prayer, Scripture, exhortation, offering, and perhaps the Lord's Supper. But no one placed these elements in a prescribed order.

Worship leaders came from the congregation. Each worshiper could perform the functions of worship. When it was discovered that specific leaders were needed and that certain of the group had particular gifts, these were set apart for definite tasks. Justin Martyr, who wrote the first detailed description of Christian worship about A.D. 145, indicated that a "president" directed the service.

The only conclusion which can be drawn is that New Testament worship was free, or fluid. It follows that Christian worship today which is consistent with the New Testament pattern will also be marked by a freedom. Orders of service should be changed occasionally to express this freedom. Indeed, many worship services need the vitality and spontaneity which come from the presence of the Spirit.

8. *Expressed in Life*

Finally, Christian worship should be expressed in life. The instruction and inspiration of worship are to eventuate in moral and ethical living which is pleasing to God. This living is not a by-product of worship; it is bound up in the nature of worship.

Worship which is not related to life will not be acceptable to God. Acts of worship which are divorced from life are rejected in the teachings of the prophets and by the Lord Jesus Christ. Amos gave classic expression to this:

I hate, I despise your feast days, and I will not smell in your solemn assemblies. Though ye offer me burnt offerings and your meat offerings, I will not accept them: neither will I regard the peace offerings of your fat beasts. Take thou away from me the noise of thy songs; for I will not hear the melody of thy viols. But let judgment run down as waters, and righteousness as a mighty stream (Amos 5:21–24).

Our Lord uttered words with the same import:

So if you are offering your gift at the altar, and there remember that your brother has something against you, leave your gift there before the altar and go; first be reconciled to your brother, and then come and offer your gift (Matt. 5:23–24, RSV).

Jesus also said, "Not everyone that saith unto me, Lord, Lord, shall enter into the kingdom of heaven; but he that doeth the will of my Father which is in heaven" (Matt. 7:21).

Those who insist that worship and living should be separated have missed the whole point of the Christian's relation to his God. Once a man is "in Christ," he is no longer his own. He is "bought with a price." Every action, even the most trivial, is to bring honor to God. "So, whether you eat or drink, or whatever you do, do all to the glory of God" (1 Cor. 10:31, RSV).

To divorce worship from life is to separate what God joined together. Worship which is unrelated to what people say, how they live, and what they think is an abomination to God. On the other hand, worship which expresses itself in Christian living is pleasing to God.

This examination of definitions and characteristics of worship can contribute to a greater understanding of the meaning of worship. But each worshiper should arrive at his own ideas. Do you have a satisfying definition? That which you believe about worship will determine the quality of worship experiences for you.

NOTES

[1] New York: The Macmillan Co., 1927, p. 164.

[2] *The Public Worship of God* (Philadelphia: The Westminster Press, 1946), pp. 15–26.

[3] *The Hope of a New World* (New York: Macmillan Co., 1942), p. 30.

[4] *Worship and Congregation* (Richmond: John Knox Press, 1963), p. 15.

[5] *Ibid.*

[6] Ilion T. Jones, *A Historical Approach to Evangelical Worship* (New York: Abingdon Press, 1954), p. 168.

[7] *Preaching the Word of God* (New York: Charles Scribner's Sons, 1943), p. 175.

[8] *Ibid.*, p. 189.

QUESTIONS TO STIMULATE DISCUSSION

1. What is your definition of worship? If you have never worked out such a definition, prepare it for class discussion.

2. Why do we hear so few sermons on the general subject of Christian worship?

3. What is the biblical meaning of worship?

4. Is worship, which is divorced from life, pleasing to God? Why?

5. How may we make worship acceptable to God and personally satisfying?

CHAPTER 3 OUTLINE

I. THE HERITAGE OF PUBLIC WORSHIP
  1. From Judaism
  2. From Apostolic Worship

II. SOME SUGGESTIONS FOR PLANNING PUBLIC WORSHIP
  1. Elements of Worship
  2. Principles of Planning

III. SOME COUNSELS FOR MAKING PUBLIC WORSHIP MORE MEANINGFUL
  1. Preparation
  2. Participation
  3. Reverence

IV. THE SETTING OF WORSHIP

3

The Congregation at Worship

THE IMPORTANCE AND NATURE OF WORSHIP have been examined. The next step will be to study the congregation at worship. It must be pleasing to God for his people to gather in his presence in a place dedicated to his worship. Their adoration, their prayers and praise, and their communion with him must be a sweet fragrance to him.

What should characterize the congregation at worship? How should corporate worship be planned? Where should it take place? What are the historical antecedents of present-day worship? Answers to these questions will help a congregation to enter more meaningfully into public worship.

I. THE HERITAGE OF PUBLIC WORSHIP

Present-day congregational worship has been influenced by many things. The primary biblical antecedents of evangelical worship come from the practices of Judaism and the apostolic church.

1. *From Judaism*

Christian worship is primarily and deeply indebted to Hebrew worship. The Master and his disciples worshiped in the Temple, which Herod had rebuilt, and in the synagogues. When Jesus returned to his native Nazareth, he went to the synagogue on the sabbath day (Luke 4:16). Until its destruction in A.D. 70, the early Christians shared in the worship in the Temple. After its destruction, even though the rift was growing between the Jews and the followers of Jesus, Christians continued to worship in the synagogues. It was through the medium of the Jewish communities that Paul and others began their witness to the pagan world. From the synagogues in the Jewish colonies around the Roman Empire, the Christian message was launched. Judaism provided more than a backdrop for the Christian faith; it furnished the stage. Quite naturally, as the new faith separated from the old, it took worship patterns and forms with it.

Though worship in the Temple did not make a major contribution to the new faith, it left its imprint. The most important feature of the Temple worship was the offering of sacrifice. Various kinds of sacrifices had developed even before the destruction of Solomon's Temple and the Exile. The idea of an offering was carried over into Christian worship. However, the biggest contribution of Temple worship to Christian worship was in the use of psalms as praise. The psalms were recited; they were sung; they were chanted. This significant element of praise was bequeathed to the church.

However, it was from the synagogue, rather than from the Temple, that Christian worship was to receive its greatest contribution. When Solomon's Temple was destroyed and the Jewish people were carried into captivity, a new means of worship had to be devised. A system of sacrifice could no longer be fulfilled. The prophets had long demanded a sacrifice of the heart and of the life. They had insisted that obedience to God's commands would be more acceptable to him than sacrifice. As the synagogue became an established part of Jewish life, the teaching of the Law and the Prophets became central in worship. The chest for the keeping of the scrolls was the new ark.

The synagogue worship which developed was quite simple. Unlike the ornate Temple, the synagogue was a simple building. Instead of a highly organized priesthood, the ruler of the synagogue shared the worship leadership with members of the congregation. Along with the reading of the Scriptures, an almost informal service of praise, prayer, and exhortation developed. The congregation participated in the praise, the prayer, and also the recitation of the Decalogue (Ten Commandments) and the Shema (Deut. 6:4–9), a declaration of faith. The *Amen* was a congregational response.

2. *From Apostolic Worship*

When the early Christians began to develop their own distinctive worship, this worship was patterned after synagogue worship. The worship consisted of the reading of the Scriptures—usually from writings of the prophets and apostles —and of exhortation, praise, prayer, and offering. In addition, there was the initiatory rite of baptism and the Lord's Supper. "They continued stedfastly in the apostle's doctrine and fellowship, and in breaking of bread, and in prayers. . . . Praising God, and having favour with all the people" (Acts 2:42-47). This is an excellent description of New Testament worship.

Justin Martyr gives the first detailed description of Sunday worship in his *First Apology*.

And on the day called Sunday there is an assembling together of all who dwell in the cities or country; and the memoirs of the apostles or the writings of the prophets are read as long as circumstances permit. Then, when the reader has ceased, the president delivers a discourse, in which he admonishes and exhorts (all present) to the imitation of these good things. Then we all rise together and pray; and, as we before said, prayer being ended, bread and wine and water are brought, and the president offers prayers in like manner, and thanksgivings, with his utmost power; and the people express their assent by saying "Amen"; and the distribution of that over which the thanksgiving has been pronounced takes place to each, and each partakes, and a portion is sent to the absent by the deacons. And they who are wealthy, and choose, give as much as they respectively deem fit; and whatever is collected is deposited with the president.[1]

New Testament worship was simple and informal. The orders were fluid, not fixed. Participation by the people was the general practice, not the exception. No evangelical Christian should apologize for participating in or for conducting worship which corrresponds to the earliest Christian practices.

II. SOME SUGGESTIONS FOR PLANNING PUBLIC WORSHIP

To accept the freedom of New Testament worship as a pattern places an extra responsibility upon those who plan and lead worship. To insist upon freedom and informality should not encourage license or formlessness. To say that Christian worship should be fluid and variable does not mean that it should be haphazard and chaotic.

How should worship be planned so that it will be most helpful to those who participate? How can a leader of worship take the primary materials—Scripture passages, prayers, music (hymns, anthems, instruments), sermon, and offering—and blend them into a satisfying worship experience? The answer to these questions is that there is no way to arrange or to plan worship, but there are certain elements of worship and certain principles which will give guidance in planning.

1. *Elements of Worship*

In recent years, considerable thought has been given to the following moods, or elements, of worship. While the suggestions vary, certain moods appear in most of the lists which have been compiled.

(1) *Recognition.*—The first element is the most difficult to express. The briefest and most exact way to express it is simply—*God*. A service of worship should begin with a sense of God, a turning to God, a recognition of God. Many Baptist worship services are weak at this point. They often begin with the rather abrupt announcement of a hymn; yet there are various ways to center attention upon God.

A prelude should create an atmosphere for worship. A call to worship, whether sung or spoken, asks the congregation to worship. An invocation, which seeks the blessing of God, recognizes God. The singing of a doxology such as Gloria Patri may help the service to begin with a sense of God.

(2) *Praise.*—With the realization of the presence of God comes the sense of joy and exaltation. Praise of God is an essential mood in worship. This praise is expressed primarily by hymns or other music. A doxology, such as Gloria Patri or the Sanctus, may be used to give voice to praise. Also, it may be expressed by appropriate responsive readings or other Scripture readings. Praise may also be and should be expressed in prayer.

(3) *Confession.*—After the spontaneous praise of God that arises from the sensing of his presence, the next element of worship may be confession. When man realizes the presence of God, he is aware of his own unworthiness. This confession may be best expressed in prayer, in hymn or anthem, or by means of a period of silence in which each worshiper may confess his own sin.

(4) *Illumination.*—Another mood of worship is illumination. The heart of the worshiper is ready to receive new light and guidance. This comes from the Scriptures and the message. God speaks through his Word and through his messenger. The Holy Spirit illumines the mind of the worshiper.

(5) *Dedication.*—The previous moods are climaxed by dedication. To encounter God, to be moved in mind and heart, is to offer oneself to God. In most Baptist services, the opportunity to express this new consecration and resolution is in the invitation. Here response may be made. Also, the offering may be an outlet for dedication.

It is possible that several of these moods may be found in the same part of the service—for example, in the prayers or the sermon. Since individual worshipers respond differently, it is difficult to determine just what mood will be created by a particular part of the service. The important thing is that these great moods be expressed in each order of worship.

2. *Principles of Planning*

After the worship leader has in mind the parts of the worship service and the moods that characterize worship, what principles should guide the planning of the service? The basic qualities of good arrangement apply to the planning of an order of service.

(1) *Unity.*—One quality of planning is unity. The service should be one service. This does not mean that there will not be varied materials, elements, and moods. It does not mean that the service will have a sense of oneness or wholeness. This unity may be derived from following a central theme, such as peace, thanksgiving, or grace. Many services are centered in one major theme. However, because of the different needs of various members of the congregation, this type of planning is not wise for most services. Generally, the single purpose, to worship God in spirit and truth, will provide sufficient unity. Though varied materials are used, they center in the general thought expressed in the Scriptures and sermon. Even with diversity of material and mood, a dominant objective will provide unity.

(2) *Order.*—Another quality of good planning is order. While unity describes the service as a whole, order has to do with the relation of the parts of the service to each other. The very desire to plan generally will bring a semblance of order to a service. To follow the different moods of worship will also give order to the service. The heading "Order of Service," given to the parts of the worship service, implies that order is essential. While any order should be subject to variation and change, God is a God of order. And order should characterize his worship.

(3) *Proportion.*—Another quality of good planning is proportion. The various parts of the service should be balanced. Each part of the service should be given the proportion of the worship time that its importance demands. If the entire serv-

ice is to be approximately sixty minutes, a proportionate time should be given the praise, prayers, Scripture reading, sermon, and other parts of the service. Generally, the pastor determines the length of the message and then gives proper time to the other parts of the service. The amount of time given to each part of the service may vary somewhat Sunday by Sunday. However, if one part of the service is out of proportion, then each part of the service and the entire service is affected.

(4) *Movement.*—Another quality of good planning is movement, or progress. The service should move forward. A printed order of service indicates this, with one part coming quickly after the other part. The movement is usually provided by the leader, who announces each part and gives the service a sense of continuing progress. A service that has a planned order from the call to worship to the invitation will usually be marked by progress.

(5) *Climax.*—The climax is one of the most important elements in worship planning. Since the sermon, ideally conceived, is where God speaks to his people through the pastor, the climax of the sermon is generally the climax of the service. However, in many Baptist services, an even greater sense of climax comes in the invitation where response to the truth is made.

(6) *Variety.*—The quality of variety is the hallmark of free or informal worship. The order of service should be flexible and may be changed from service to service. Some people who do not like form, or liturgy, use the same order of service year after year. These people have unknowingly developed their own liturgy, for liturgy means order of service. Baptist churches should change their order of service frequently, if only to express their free worship tradition. Worship services planned with variety and flexibility are usually more interesting than fixed orders.

These various qualities can be used to arrange the parts

of the service. These parts of the service will be discussed
in detail in later chapters.

III. Some Counsels for Making Public Worship More Meaningful

Along with these specific suggestions, some general counsels may contribute to more meaningful worship.

1. *Preparation*

To be most meaningful, worship requires preparation. It
is taken for granted that the leaders will prepare the service
according to the principles suggested previously. The worship leaders and the worshipers also should prepare themselves. Some of this preparation should be physical. People
may attend worship with weary bodies and tired minds. They
half drift and half sleep through the worship; they are semi-
conscious in the presence of God. Such attempts at worship
must be an abomination to God.

However, the major preparation to be made is spiritual.
Each worshiper should prepare his mind and heart. By meditation, prayer, and new commitment, the worshiper places
himself in a stream of love where he may experience new
spiritual power.

What would happen to many services if the participants
prayed for the presence of the Holy Spirit to come upon the
waiting congregation? Surely a new reality would pervade
the worship.

2. *Participation*

A most important factor in worship is participation. Actually, genuine worship demands participation. The moment
a participant in a service becomes a spectator, he ceases to
be a worshiper. In some services, most of the people are
spectators; they observe and appraise the worship rather
than share in it.

These members of the congregation withdraw to criticize and evaluate. They take note of the appearance of the choir and the mannerisms of the preacher. They do not sing, they do not pray, and they may not listen to the sermon. These people may be classed as spectators, rather than worshipers.

Genuine worship calls for active participation. Each worshiper should say: "The hymn is my hymn; I will sing. The prayer is my prayer; I will offer it to God. The Scripture passage is God's Word; I will let him speak. The sermon is God's message to me; I will listen." This attitude makes worship meaningful.

3. Reverence

Reverential awe is still a basic attitude in sincere worship. The Lord God is being worshiped. Now is the time to lay the cares, concerns, and conversations of daily life aside. Many people bring into the sanctuary the chatter from the street. Some people continue this after the prelude begins, and some even after the first part of the worship is announced. Others simply let their minds wander and are far from God. To be in God's house and to be oblivious of his presence is almost sacrilege.

God is God. There are no gods like him. He is worthy of the highest recognition. To be in the presence of the King of the universe should inspire awe and wonder. To worship God truly is to worship him with our minds, to offer him our best attention. It must be meaningful to God when he sees his people bowing quietly and humbly before him. Without real reverence, meaningful worship is impossible.

IV. THE SETTING OF WORSHIP

The heritage of worship, suggestions for planning worship, and counsels about corporate worship have been discussed. The physical setting of worship should be observed now.

Until approximately A.D. 200, Christians did not have buildings or places for worship. The people met in upper rooms, caves, and tombs—wherever they could meet without interference. When Christian houses of worship were built, they were simple in structure as the synagogue had been. The pattern followed was the rectangular Roman basilica, an oblong hall. Ornate buildings soon evolved, but the original building was simple.

Although church buildings today are varied in structure, most churches build simply. Only a few congregations invest large sums of money in elaborate structures. Actually, ornate and luxurious buildings are incompatible with the compelling needs of the world and the missionary purpose of the church. A simply constructed meetinghouse may be adequate for the needs of the congregation.

Attention should be given to the symbolism within the church. This symbolism should not deny the theological concepts of the congregation. Most Baptists believe that the Word of God should be central in worship. This means that the pulpit will be central for the reading and proclamation of God's Word. To make an altar central and to put the pulpit to one side gives a symbolic picture that most Baptists do not accept. Having the pulpit and the table together suggests a balance between the Word and the Supper. A raised pulpit indicates that preaching is the primary act of worship. Southern Baptists should not allow the beauty of a divided chancel to cause them to adopt a symbolism that denies their basic theological belief.

Perhaps these suggestions will help to make the corporate, or public, worship of Southern Baptists more worthwhile and meaningful.

NOTES

[1] John Kaye, *The Ancient & Modern Library of Theological Literature: Justin Martyr's Apology* (London: Griffith Farran Okeden & Welsh), p. 67.

QUESTIONS TO STIMULATE DISCUSSION

1. In what ways did synagogue worship influence Christian worship?

2. What are the worship patterns of other denominations?

3. What suggestions would you have for planning and conducting a worship service?

4. In what ways does your building promote or hinder a worshipful spirit?

CHAPTER 4 OUTLINE

I. THE BIBLE READ
   1. The Place for the Scriptures
   2. The Uses of the Bible in Worship
   3. Suggestions for Scripture Reading

II. THE BIBLE PROCLAIMED
   1. The Centrality of Preaching
   2. The Nature of the Sermon
   3. The Sermon as Worship
   4. The Sermon and the Supper
   5. The Congregation's Part in the Preaching

4

The Bible in Worship

THE SCRIPTURES HAVE ALWAYS BEEN essential in Christian worship. When the first Christians met for worship, they read selections from the Old Testament. Then, as the Gospels and Epistles were written, these were read. As the various books were collected into the Bible, the reading and exhortation from this book formed a basic part of early Christian worship.

It is easy to understand why this was true. One aspect of worship is communion—man speaks to God, and God speaks to man. It is in the reading and proclamation of his Word that God speaks most clearly to his people.

I. THE BIBLE READ

Since a part of Christian worship is to hear God's Word, the reading of the Scriptures should be an essential part of any worship patterned after the New Testament.

1. *The Place for the Scriptures*

Is the reading of the Bible given a significant place in Southern Baptist worship today? Much evidence reveals that the reading of the Scriptures is given a minimal place. Often only a brief passage of Scripture is read, and this is read at one point in the service. Scripture reading deserves and demands more attention than this. If God is to speak, he must be given the opportunity. Rather than reading just a brief text, it would be well to read the context and perhaps the entire chapter containing the text.

Some denominations follow the Christian year and use a

lectionary, or list of readings, as a guide for Scripture reading. Two Scripture passages, one from the Old Testament and one from the New Testament, are read in each service. This pattern of reading has advantages. It provides adequate Scripture reading in each service, and it keeps before the congregation God's redemptive acts in Christ.

Since Southern Baptists do not use a lectionary as a guide for Scripture reading, some other plan should be devised to give the reading of the Word of God a more significant place in public worship. There could be two readings in each service—one embodying the preacher's text and one additional reading. A portion of some book of the Bible may be read Sunday by Sunday until the book is completed. Also, the *Baptist Hymnal* has one hundred and two responsive readings that could be used for at least a year. After a lapse of time, these responsive readings could be used again. But regardless of the method used for doing it, the Word of God must be read. Scripture reading was an important part of early church worship; this pattern should be recovered today. As will be noted later, the reading of the Bible has been one of the central elements in private and family worship also.

2. *The Uses of the Bible in Worship*

A review of the many ways the Bible may be used in a service will provide some answers.

(1) *Calls to worship.*—Calls to worship come from many sources, but the best and most frequently used source is the Bible. Calls to worship may be found in different books of the Bible, but the book of Psalms is the richest treasury. Calls to worship taken from the Bible, though brief, will add Scripture use to the service.

(2) *Offertory sentences.*—Another use of the Scriptures is the offertory sentence. Excellent passages from both the Old and New Testaments may be quoted before the offering. A minister can make a collection of these passages. As the

passages of Scripture are quoted again and again, they become familiar to the congregation. In addition to adding Scripture use to the service, these passages offer biblical teaching on Christian stewardship.

(3) *Benedictions.*—Another way to use the Scriptures in the service is the biblical benediction. A biblical benediction may be the best way to close a service. These benedictions are few, may be memorized easily, and may be found in any pastors' manual. They do not need additions, but should be quoted as they are recorded in the Bible. The Aaronic blessing (Num. 6:22–27) and the Pauline benedictions (Rom. 16:24; 2 Cor. 13:14; Gal. 6:18; Eph. 6:23; 1 Tim. 6:20–21) are the most frequently used benedictions.

(4) *The responsive reading.*—The responsive reading is one of the best methods of bringing more Scripture reading into a service. Because they are adaptable to themes and seasons, responsive readings are especially helpful. If the hymnbook does not have a sufficient variety of readings, chapters of the Bible may be read responsively. Responsive readings not only add Scripture use to the service, but they allow participation by the congregation.

(5) *Additional Scripture reading.*—In order to increase the reading of the Bible, some pastors are reading another passage of Scripture. Some read an Old Testament lesson and a New Testament lesson. Others read through a book of the Bible. Since the reading of the Bible is so important, two readings in a service would be more appropriate than one.

(6) *Scripture reading.*—The main use of the Scriptures in the service has been the Scripture lesson, which is the basis for the sermon. In recent years, this lesson has become brief. However, the renewed emphasis on expository preaching has started a new trend. No pastor should apologize for a long Scripture reading. The Bible is the Word of God. It is the source of authority for evangelicals. It is the rule of faith and practice, and it should be heard gladly.

The bidding "Hear the Word of God" needs to be re-emphasized. It may be worthwhile to revive an early church custom and have the people stand for the reading of the Scripture passages, especially the Gospels. However it is done, the reading of the Bible must be magnified.

3. Suggestions for Scripture Reading

Since many people read the Bible in various worship and departmental services, some suggestions for this reading will be helpful.

(1) *Locate the reading.*—Since many worshipers desire to follow the reading in their Bibles, the worship leader should announce and locate the Scripture reading. It is quite frustrating to many listeners to hear the Bible read and yet not know the book, chapter, and verse. Time should be taken to identify and locate the Scripture passages. If the hearers have Bibles with them, they can follow the reading. If not, they will know from which book it is taken and will not miss the reading by trying to identify it. If the Authorized Version is not being used, the translation being used should be identified.

(2) *Make it audible.*—Since the Scripture passage is read for others to hear, it must be audible. A reader cannot read the Bible for a large group in the same manner that he would read it for a small group. A public reading must be heard to have value. Therefore, when the Bible is read, the reader should lift up his head and lift up his voice. The Word of God is to be heard.

(3) *Read with understanding.*—The meaning of the passage should be made clear to the congregation. The Bible should be read with understanding in order that its meaning may be transmitted. It follows that the Scripture verses must be studied carefully. What does the passage mean?

Then, the reader should practice reading the chosen verses. In fact, no Scripture passage should be read publicly that has not been read aloud privately at least twice. When Ezra and the scribes read the Law, it was recorded: "They read in the book in the law of God distinctly, and gave the sense, and caused them to understand the reading" (Neh. 8:8). This biblical example of Scripture reading should be followed today.

(4) *Do not overread.*—The worship leader should not overly dramatize the reading of the Scripture passage. The reading should not take attention away from the Bible, but rather it should call attention to it. When the reading is finished, the hearer's exclamation should not be, "What a wonderful reader!" but rather, "How wonderful is God's Word!" W. E. Sangster gives excellent advice for Scripture reading: "The extremes to avoid are slovenliness on the one hand, and exaggerated elocution on the other." [1] The Bible should not be elocuted, but read with meaningful emphasis. It has worth of its own that, given the opportunity, will speak for itself.

The Bible can be God's voice to his people. It should be read with great purpose and seriousness. In and through the reading of God's Word, he speaks to his people.

II. THE BIBLE PROCLAIMED

God not only speaks through the reading of the Scriptures, but he speaks through the sermon. He speaks through the man whom he has called. Preaching in the highest sense is God confronting his people through his preacher.

1. *The Centrality of Preaching*

The Christian faith gave a central place to preaching which it never enjoyed before. Philosophies had their orators. Judaism had its occasional preachers. But only with Christianity did the people regularly congregate to hear the proclamation of a message.

Indeed, the Gospels were first proclamations. The redemptive acts of God were proclaimed to a lost world before the Holy Spirit brooded upon the minds and hearts of men and inspired them to record God's saving message.

Preaching should have a prominent place. Jesus came preaching. He was a traveling preacher whom the common people heard gladly. He commanded his disciples to preach, and they went everywhere preaching the good news. Before Jesus ascended to the Father, he commissioned all of his followers to witness and to preach. It was the Master's divine intention that his disciples declare his redemptive acts and that, when men heard, they put their faith in him and know the joy of his salvation. Paul caught the essence of this when he said: "How then shall they call on him in whom they have not believed? and how shall they believe in him of whom they have not heard? and how shall they hear without a preacher?" (Rom. 10:14).

Preaching was to be God's chief way to bring the message of salvation to a lost world. When the church has forgotten this, it has lost its outreach. When it has remembered this and relied upon preaching, the church has been strong.

One of the tragedies of Southern Baptist life is that some churches and pastors have made preaching secondary. Perhaps without intending to do so, some churches make so many demands upon a pastor that he does not have the time to prepare for preaching. A recent survey of more than four thousand ministers revealed that their greatest problem is that they do not have time to pray or to study. Some preachers actually have lost faith in their preaching. They no longer believe that something can happen in the act of preaching. They feel that no decisions will be made in the service that have not been made before the service. They seem to have forgotten that God's chief means of saving men has been by the "foolishness of preaching."

The early church gave an exalted place to preaching. Today, the sermon receives the most time in the service. Yet, apparently it is not considered the most important part of the preacher's work. If the church is to pulsate with spiritual power, churches and preachers must see anew the pre-eminence of preaching.

2. The Nature of the Sermon

If preaching is so important, the real nature of the sermon must be understood. What is the sermon? It is a discourse setting forth the mind of God. Ideally, the sermon does not set forth ideas, thoughts, and opinions of the preacher. Rather, it proclaims the message of God. The Lord's declaration "For as the heavens are higher than the earth, so are my ways higher than your ways, and my thoughts than your thoughts" (Isa. 55:9) is especially true of the sermon. To see preaching as an exposition of the Scriptures is to have the highest concept of preaching.

Here the close relationship between the Scripture text and the sermon is seen. The sermon is based on the Scripture passage. Illustration, amplification, and application may come from many sources, but the key ideas come from the Word of God. In a sense, preaching is giving the Bible a voice. Donald Miller has insisted "that all true preaching is expository preaching, and that preaching which is not expository is not preaching." [2] This may be an overstatement. Preaching may be biblical that is not expository. But the stress is correct. The Bible is read that it may be heard and proclaimed. In reality, a sermon that is not biblical is not homiletical because a homily is a talk based on the Scriptures.

God speaks through the sermon. The minister has studied God's Word and learned God's message. Now, he proclaims this message to the waiting congregation.

3. The Sermon as Worship

What is the relationship of the sermon to the parts of the worship service? Is the sermon worship? Is it an intruder in worship? Is it the only true worship? Different answers to these questions are given by various denominations. Three views are widely held concerning the place of the sermon in worship.

(1) *Some say the sermon is not worship.*—Some Christians think that the sermon is not worship. They think the sermon is an intrusion in the service. It may be tolerated, but only for custom's sake. In a few isolated instances, some worshipers have left when the sermon began. Some denominations, especially the Anglican and Roman Catholic, have omitted the sermon from the order of service. However, few evangelical Christians consider the sermon to be an intrusion.

(2) *Some say the sermon is all-important.*—Many view the sermon as an isolated sovereign to which all the rest of the church must do obeisance. The sermon is all-important. Some who arrive late for a service feel they have not "missed anything" if the sermon has not begun. Others will not attend a service when a sermon is not to be preached. Both laymen and preachers talk about "the preliminaries." Even thoughtful people talk about "preaching and worship" or the "sermon and worship." No such division should exist. While the sermon is the central act of worship, other parts of the service are worship, too.

(3) *The sermon is an act of worship.*—What is the proper place of the sermon in the service? It is an integral part of the worship. It is an act of worship itself. While it is the most important part of the service, it is not the only part. The hymns, the prayers, the Scripture reading, and the offering are also worship. The sermon is first among equals. It should be primary and climactic, but it does not stand alone. It is one act of worship in a service of worship.

Since preaching is the proclamation of God's message, any attempt to separate preaching and worship misses the basic meaning of both. In worship, God speaks and man hears. As his minister preaches, God speaks. This is true worship.

4. *The Sermon and the Supper*

At several points in this chapter, the sermon has been called the central act of worship. Many worship leaders in other denominations would emphatically disagree with this. They would insist strongly that the central act of worship is the Lord's Supper, or the Eucharist. Most books on the theory of Christian worship assume this position.

Without downgrading the Lord's Supper or denying the injunction "This do in remembrance of me," the last commands which Jesus gave his disciples seemed to center in preaching, in sharing the goods news of his redemptive acts. The Lord's Supper is one means of "proclaiming the Lord's death. It is not the only means. It does not appear from the New Testament record to be the primary means.

Jesus himself fulfilled the role of a prophet, rather than the role of a priest. He preached and taught, and he called his disciples to do the same thing. God through his Son, and not the Supper, is the source of grace and salvation. As other heresies evolved, so did the heresy that the elements of the Supper become the actual flesh and blood of Christ and that these elements give forgiveness to the receivers.

The fairest relationship between the sermon and the Supper may be that of balance. Both have a place in worship. Many evangelicals convey something of this symbolism in their church buildings. The pulpit and the table are together. The pulpit probably is elevated above the table. This elevation, if symbolic of the central place of the Scriptures and the sermon, may be correct. It is much more symbolic of true biblical doctrine than a divided chancel with a central altar. In the upper rooms of the New Testament Christians, a table was probably both the pulpit and the table. Some evangelical groups may need to give the Supper a more prominent place, without letting it supercede or replace preaching. Rightly understood, the Supper is one way of preaching the redemptive acts of God.

5. *The Congregation's Part in the Preaching*

The congregation has a responsible part to fulfil in the preaching of the gospel. This part is more than a response to the preaching.

It may begin with the hearer's concept of the preacher and his task. The preacher should be accepted as a man called of God to a specific task. He is to proclaim God's message. This message should be received by God's people as his message to them. This exalted concept of the preacher's task will cause a congregation to listen with more understanding and obedience.

The congregation should pray constantly for the preacher. The members should pray that he will find God's message and that he will declare it with conviction and power. No one should criticize the preacher who has not first prayed for him. To pray for the preacher is to participate in his preaching.

In addition to praying for the preacher, the congregation should listen reverently, prayerfully, and expectantly. Why is it easy to preach for one congregation and extremely difficult to preach for another? The difference is often in the attitude of the congregation. Some congregations bear the preacher up, while others stifle preaching.

Finally, the congregation should respond to the preaching. Assuming that God's message is proclaimed, it must be believed and obeyed. A message from God's Word must have a positive response from every true believer.

Thus the Bible has an important place in worship. As the Bible is read, the worshiper hears the word of God. As the Bible is proclaimed, the worshiper find God's message related to his life.

NOTES

[1] *The Approach to Preaching* (Philadelphia: The Westminster Press, 1952), p. 71.
[2] *The Way to Biblical Preaching* (Nashville: Abingdon Press, 1957), p. 22.

QUESTIONS TO STIMULATE DISCUSSION

1. If you have a sixty-minute service, how many minutes are given to Scripture reading?

2. There are many translations of the Bible. Should these be used in the public reading of the Scriptures?

3. Does your church have a pulpit Bible? If so, is it used? If not, why not?

4. Is preaching (the sermon) the most important part of the worship service? Why, or why not?

5. Should every sermon have a text? Why, or why not?

6. How may the congregation contribute to the preaching?

CHAPTER 5 OUTLINE

5

Prayer in Worship

PRAYER HAS BEEN CALLED the soul of worship. Though this is an exalted claim for prayer, it may not be an overstatement. Prayer, more than other parts of worship, captures the essence of worship. It recognizes God because it addresses him. It communes with God because communion with God is its reason for being. It is offering because the Christian cannot really converse with God and withhold from him.

Prayer has always been an essential part of Christian worship. It has been the major facet of private devotion, and it has been a significant part of public worship. In a typical Sunday morning worship service, eight to ten minutes may be given to prayer. Since private worship will be discussed in chapter 7, this chapter will deal primarily with prayer in the public worship.

I. THE NATURE OF PUBLIC PRAYER

The nature of public prayer is often misunderstood. Public prayer is more than private prayer. In private prayer, a Christian is under no special restraints. He is in conversation with his Lord and may follow his own moods. But in public prayer, the leader is doing more than offering a private prayer in public. He is attempting to offer a prayer for all the people. Public prayer is a corporate act; the one prayer is made in behalf of all of those present. The leader

... is called to the delicate task of enlisting the minds, consciences, aspirations, and wills of a heterogeneous collection of people in one corporate act of dedication. He must speak for them ... and

53

he must make it possible for them in their hearts to be at one with him as he addresses the Most High God in their behalf.[1]

The leader of prayer is faced with an awesome responsibility. His prayer must be more than a monologue to which the people listen. It must so catch the common petitions and desires of the people that they actually share in it. In corporate prayer, the leader utters the words, but the congregation prays. Public prayer is common prayer; the minister is to offer the prayers of the whole congregation.

This high purpose cannot be done in any careless, haphazard fashion. The conduct of corporate prayer is an art. The more knowledge a leader has of the task, the more likely he is to fulfil his grave responsibility.

II. THE ELEMENTS OF PRAYER

Basic to any understanding of private, family, or corporate prayer is some knowledge of the elements of prayer.

1. *Adoration*

The keynote of prayer, indeed of all true worship, is adoration. This is the sheer praise of God. He is given the glory due unto his name. This gives objectivity to prayer. It begins where it should begin, not with man and his need, but with God whom man loves and who is worthy of his worship. However, in spite of its importance, this element is often lacking in public prayer.

2. *Thanksgiving*

Prayer moves easily from adoration to thanksgiving. To praise God is to be reminded of his loving-kindness. The worshiper knows how dependent he is upon God. He recalls the many gifts of God. Especially does he remember the "unspeakable gift," the gift of Jesus Christ. Gratitude for God's grace should be the climax of thanksgiving. Grace and gratitude actually came to us from the same word, *charis.* Grace in the heart will mean gratitude on the lips.

3. *Confession*

Another element of prayer is confession. To be in the holy presence of God is to be aware of one's sin. Confession of sin brings reconciliation and peace with God. A part of every pastoral prayer should be the confession of sin. This should be more than a general "Forgive us our sins." It should be a confession of the specific sins of the congregation in public admission.

4. *Petition*

Petition is also an element of prayer. Petition is sharing our requests with God. This element of prayer may be over-emphasized. Yet, God wants his children to make their needs known to him. Petition was a part of the prayer that Jesus taught his disciples to pray. "Give us this day our daily bread. And forgive us our debts, as we forgive our debtors. And lead us not into temptation, but deliver us from evil" (Matt. 6:11–13). Jesus taught his followers to pray with the assurance that the Heavenly Father would hear and answer. "Ask, and it shall be given you; seek, and ye shall find; knock, and it shall be opened unto you: For every one that asketh receiv-eth; and he that seeketh findeth; and to him that knocketh it shall be opened" (Matt. 7:7–8).

5. *Intercession*

Intercession is closely related to petition. It is making a request in behalf of others. This is an element of prayer which should be magnified. It lifts us out of ourselves and calls our attention to the needs of others. According to James, "The effectual fervent prayer of a righteous man availeth much" (James 5:16).

6. *Dedication*

Still another element of prayer is dedication, or commitment. God's people give themselves anew to him. This element of prayer is most appropriate at the offering or at the end of the sermon. To be in the presence of God is to be impelled to commit oneself to him.

Adoration, thanksgiving, confession, petition, intercession, and dedication are the primary elements of prayer. All of them need not be in every prayer, but all of them should be found in the different prayers in a service.

III. A VARIETY OF PRAYERS

Corporate prayers vary both in kind and in method. They may be classified according to their location in the service, or by the method used in offering the prayer.

1. *The Prayers of a Service*

The number of prayers in a service vary greatly, but certain prayers appear in most Sunday morning worship services. Fewer prayers are used in a typical Sunday evening service.

(1) *The invocation.*—The first prayer in a service is usually the invocation. Its primary purpose is to invoke the blessing of God upon the worship and the worshipers. It should not be an opening prayer which tends to cover all the elements of prayer and to supercede the pastoral prayer. It should briefly major on two elements, adoration and petition. It should magnify God, and it should seek his blessing on the service.

(2) *The pastoral prayer.*—The primary prayer of the service is the pastoral prayer, or the morning prayer. It is called the pastoral prayer because it is led by the pastor. In it, the shepherd of the flock offers prayer to God for all the people. This prayer is usually longer and more comprehensive than

the other prayers. It should major on thanksgiving, confession, petition, and intercession. Since the needs of the people vary from Sunday to Sunday, this prayer should vary. Some pastors, while opposing form, offer the same prayer service after service.

(3) *The offertory prayer.*—The offertory prayer is so named because it is related to the offering, or giving. It generally precedes the offering, but it may follow. This prayer offers an excellent prayer opportunity to express dedication and commitment. It often begins with thanksgiving, but majors on dedication of the people and their gifts to God.

(4) *The prayer after the sermon.*—A prayer which is increasing in use is the prayer after the sermon. Many pastors are using this prayer. It may be a sermon conclusion, or it may be a prayer of petition and commitment. The prayer may ask that the sermon's purpose be fulfilled, or the pastor may offer himself and his people to God in a new act of dedication.

(5) *The benediction.*—The final prayer is commonly termed the benediction. In actual practice, this is a closing prayer which may review the entire service. However, this should be a brief prayer. If a prayer has been offered after the sermon, a biblical benediction can appropriately close the service. These are true benedictions, or "blessings of God upon the people," and they have the added advantage of being brief.

2. *The Ways of Praying*

Not only are there different kinds of prayer, but corporate prayer may be expressed in a variety of ways.

(1) *Extemporaneous prayer.*—Extemporaneous, or "free," prayer is the most commonly used method of prayer. This prayer is uttered as it comes to the person praying in the moment of delivery. He may have a general organization which he follows, but the objects of thanks, the sins con-

fessed, the petitions, and the intercessions are those which come to the mind of the pastor as the prayer is offered.

Spontaneous prayer is the kind of prayer found in the New Testament and in the very early church. It is used, and will continue to be used, in Baptist churches. Any evangelical pastor or deacon should be able to lead a congregation in prayer when called upon to do so. The disadvantage of the extemporaneous method is that it may lack order, and the same elements and objects of prayer may be repeated service after service. Extemporaneous prayer often may be disorganized and irrelevant.

(2) *Planned public prayer.*—The corporate prayers may be prepared. The minister decides what elements and objects he will use in the different prayers in the service. He may prepare an outline, or he may write the prayer in detail. In common practice, few Southern Baptist ministers write their prayers, and still fewer read them. But planned public prayer generally can be more intelligible and meaningful to the congregation.

(3) *The collect.*—Another method of public prayer is the collect. This is an opening prayer, and it probably can be found in one of the historic liturgies. It also may be contemporary. The Lord's Prayer is an example of a collect. Another classic example is the beautiful invocation taken from the Gregorian Sacramentary:

Almighty God, unto whom all hearts be open, all desires known, and from whom no secrets are hid, cleanse the thoughts of our hearts by the inspiration of thy Holy Spirit, that we may perfectly love thee, and worthily magnify thy holy name; through Christ our Lord. Amen.

Many other usable collects are found in compilations of public prayer. The use of a collect occasionally can offer some variety to the prayers of a worship service.

(4) *The litany.*—Another method of corporate prayer is the litany. In a litany, the minister offers a petition and the con-

gregation responds. This type of prayer may be printed in the order of service. T. B. McDormand offers a prayer on "Thanksgiving" as an example of a litany.[2]

LEADER: Eternal God, giver of every good and perfect gift, for thine infinite love made known to men in creation and in the wondrous plan of salvation in thy Son, Jesus Christ our Lord,

GROUP: Hear our thanksgiving, O Lord.

LEADER: For the beauty and fertility of the earth, providing food for the body and soul of thy children.

GROUP: Hear our thanksgiving, O Lord.

LEADER: For the sure succession of the seasons, with their infinite variety of wonder and beauty, and with their constant witness to thy power and providence,

GROUP: Hear our thanksgiving, O Lord.

LEADER: For thy love for sinful, weak, and erring humanity, and for the gracious provision of a Saviour through whom we can, by faith, become more than conquerors over sin and death,

GROUP: Hear our thanksgiving, O Lord.

LEADER: For the ever present help and guidance of thy Holy Spirit, through whom we overcome temptation, discover and follow the way of eternal life, behold and ever seek after the City of God,

GROUP: Hear our thanksgiving, O Lord.

LEADER: Let us conclude our prayer by uniting in the words of the Lord's Prayer.

Southern Baptists engage in this kind of prayer on special occasions such as the dedication of a sanctuary. Litanies could be used more often and would allow the congregation another avenue of participation in the service.

(5) *Bidding prayer.*—Still another way of praying is bidding prayer. This kind of prayer is guided meditation. The leader of worship will ask the congregation to keep in mind one of the elements of prayer, or to pray for some specific object. For example, the leader may say, "Let us give thanks." Or, he may say, "Let us pray for those who are sick." After each "bidding" to prayer, the leader allows time for the congregation to pray. This type of prayer lends itself to the evening service and to the prayer service. Again, the con-

gregation has an opportunity to participate. Most congregations find real spiritual blessing in bidding prayer.

(6) *Silent prayer.*—Still another method of praying is through the use of silence. The pastor or worship leader calls upon the members of the congregation to pray silently. Most congregations appreciate sharing in this kind of prayer. A caution should be observed. When the people are asked to engage in silent prayer, sufficient time should be allowed for them to pray. Some worship leaders call upon the congregation to pray and, then, do not give the members time to pray.

Corporate prayer is not limited to one kind or method. A great variety of types and ways of prayer are available to the worship leader. No evangelical church should develop a ritual by using the same kind and method of prayer continually.

IV. THE LEADERSHIP OF CORPORATE PRAYER

The nature, elements, and variety of public prayers have been discussed. Now, the leadership of public prayer will be examined.

1. *The Leaders*

Who should lead the congregation in prayer? It is normally assumed that the pastor will lead the congregation in prayer. By his pastoral work and other contacts with his people, he knows their needs and desires. He should be able to offer common prayer more adequately and effectively than anyone else. However, in Baptist churches many people share in leading corporate prayer. Other members of the staff—such as the minister of music, the minister of education, or the youth worker—may lead one or more prayers in a given service. Deacons and other laymen may lead the congregation in prayer. A guest, a visiting minister, a former member, a denominational leader, or some other guest also may be asked to lead the congregation in prayer. This variety of leaders seems to correspond with the New Testament pattern of informal prayer.

2. Qualities of Prayer

Regardless of the leader, certain qualities of prayer should be kept in mind if the congregation is to participate easily in corporate prayer.

One essential quality of corporate prayer is brevity. When people have their heads bowed and their eyes closed, it is difficult for them to maintain attention for a long time. Long prayers lose the congregation and are not effective. Remember that there are four or five prayers in most services. Each prayer, with the possible exception of the pastoral prayer, should be brief.

Order is a most important quality of public prayer. In corporate prayer, the elements and objects should not be mingled. When the leader engages in thanks, let him include all the objects. He should not give thanks, offer petition, and return to thanks. In private prayer, the person praying may just follow his meditation, but in public prayer, where many minds are involved, order is essential.

Another necessary quality is concreteness. Many prayers suffer from vague generalities. The leader gives thanks "for all of our blessings," or he calls upon the Lord to "forgive us our sins." One who prays should specify the blessings and the sins. Since there are many in each category, different ones may be cited on successive Sundays until the whole range of thanks and sins have been mentioned in prayer.

Public prayer should be comprehensive. All six elements should be experienced in the four or five prayers of the service. A variety of objects of thanks, petitions, and intercessions should be noted. Of course, not all the objects can be mentioned in one service, but they can be mentioned over a period of Sundays. Comprehensive prayer avoids the sameness found in much public prayer.

3. *Some Counsels*

Since different leaders share in public prayer, some practical counsels may prove helpful.

The voice of prayer should be heard easily. It need not be loud. Just as God does not hear the worshiper for his much speaking, neither does he hear him for his loud speaking. Yet, the prayer must be heard if it is to fulfil its purpose. The leader is offering a prayer for all of the people. If the people do not hear, they cannot participate.

Sometimes, when lay people and others are called upon to lead in prayer, the prayer is not heard. It is always better if the one leading in prayer faces the congregation. The one leading in prayer could be on the platform. Also, prayer will be heard better if the one praying will lift up his head when he begins to speak. The leader of prayer should "bow" his heart, but lift up his head and his voice in order that he may be heard.

Prayer is addressed to God. It should not be talk about God which is directed to the people. There is a time to preach and a time to pray. When prayer leaves the direct address of the second person and drops into the third person, the leader is preaching and not praying. Occasionally, a listener feels that the pastor may be concluding the sermon in prayer and telling the people something he did not have the courage to say before. Those responsible for public prayer should not use it as an occasion to preach.

Since public prayer is addressed to God, it should not be used to make announcements to the people. Some leaders of worship, forgetting to make announcements at the proper time, incorporate them into the prayer. Have you ever heard a statement like this in a morning prayer, "Lord, help our people remember the meeting this afternoon at 2:30 in the T.E.L. room"? When announcements are made or when other information is given to the congregation, prayer ceases to be prayer.

Since the name of deity is used in prayer, it should be offered in a reverent spirit. Vehemence or great force may cause some members of the congregation to feel that the minister is cursing. Also, the Holy Spirit should not be referred to as "it." If the Triune God is Father, Son, and Holy Spirit, the Spirit is "he." Prayer should never be offered in a nonchalant manner. The Lord God should be addressed reverently.

The leader should let the congregation know that he is going to pray. He should not just slip into prayer. If he suddenly begins to pray, some worshipers will participate and some will not. Others will be embarrassed when they discover that they are not participating. A leader may give a common signal for prayer, such as the outstretched arm with palm down. Or he may simply say to the people, "Let us pray." These counsels will help each leader and potential leader of prayer to pray more effectively.

NOTES

[1] Morgan Phelps Noyes, *Preaching the Word of God* (New York: Charles Scribner's Sons, 1943), p. 180.

[2] *The Art of Building Worship Services* (Nashville: Broadman Press, 1942), pp. 68–69.

QUESTIONS TO STIMULATE DISCUSSION

1. How does public prayer differ from private prayer?
2. Attention was called to six elements of prayer. Are there others? What are they?
3. What are some values of participating in bidding prayer?
4. Do you believe in preparing prayers? Should they be read?
5. Who should lead the prayers in a service?

CHAPTER 6 OUTLINE

I. OUR HERITAGE OF PRAISE THROUGH MUSIC

II. A VARIETY OF PRAISE
1. Prelude
2. Choral Call to Worship
3. Responses
4. Solo and Ensemble Music
5. Hymns

III. A VARIETY OF THEMES

IV. CHARACTERISTICS OF PRAISE THROUGH MUSIC
1. Theologically Acceptable
2. Simplicity in Form and Language
3. Singability
4. Fully Understandable

V. FUNCTIONS OF PRAISE
1. Congregational Participation
2. Creating Oneness
3. Arousing and Expressing Emotions
4. Instilling Doctrine

VI. ADVICE ABOUT PRAISE THROUGH MUSIC
1. Study the Hymnal
2. Select Hymns Which Center in God
3. Select Hymns to Meet Various Needs
4. Educate the Congregation in the Great Hymns
5. Participate in the Praise

6

Praise in Worship

THE CHRISTIAN CHURCH received a rich legacy of musical praise from Judaism, as well as a wonderful heritage of exhortation and prayer in the Scriptures. For centuries, devout Jews gave expression to their worship of the living God by singing. This singing was often accompanied by musical instruments and was shared by the entire congregation. When the Christian church took form, praise was a part of its worship. It had a pattern of congregational singing, and the Psalter was its hymnbook. Moreover, the Christian could sing many of the psalms with new meaning. The Lord God, to whom their praise was addressed, had now visited and redeemed his people in Jesus Christ.

I. OUR HERITAGE OF PRAISE THROUGH MUSIC

The Christians made immediate use of psalms. This was normal when Christians shared in synagogue worship. However, the psalms were used in distinctively Christian worship. The hymn used at the institution of the Lord's Supper—"When they had sung an hymn, they went out" (Mark 14:26)—probably was a psalm. And this practice continued.

The Christians not only sang psalms; they began immediately to develop hymns on Christian themes. Scholars feel that hymn fragments are to be found in the New Testament. The songs in Luke's Gospel, the songs of Zacharias, Mary, and Simeon—usually called the Benedictus, the Magnificat, and the Nunc Dimittis—may have been used in the worship of the early church.

Paul may be quoting a line of a hymn in his letter to the Ephesians: "Awake, sleeper, and arise from the dead, and Christ will shine on you" (Eph. 5:14, NASB). Another excerpt may be found in 1 Timothy 3:16—

> He who was revealed in the flesh,
> Was vindicated in the Spirit,
> Beheld by angels,
> Proclaimed among the nations,
> Believed on in the world,
> Taken up in glory (NASB).

Still another fragment may be seen in 2 Timothy 2:11–13—

> For if we died with him, we shall also
>   live with Him;
> If we endure, we shall also reign with Him;
> If we deny Him, He also will deny us;
> If we are faithless, He remains faithful;
>   for He cannot deny Himself (NASB).

These and other fragments suggest that a hymnody arose quite early in the life of the church.

Singing of the psalms and hymns was congregational. The congregation participated and gave voice to its praise. Some of the praise seemed to be spontaneous praise to the Lord Jesus Christ. Paul probably referred to this kind of praise when he urged the Ephesians to continue "singing and making melody in your heart to the Lord" (Eph. 5:19), and the Colossians to sing "with grace in your hearts to the Lord" (Col. 3:16).

Paul seemed to be suggesting a variety of praise when he gave the injunction of "speaking to yourselves in psalms and hymns and spiritual songs" (Eph. 5:19). Paul was referring to the Jewish psalms, to the hymns which the Christians had composed, and perhaps to the more spontaneous gospel song. The gospel song which some seem to reject today may have had a lofty origin.

As time passed, congregational singing almost ceased.

Congregational participation also was lost. With the exception of some of the evangelical sects, the medieval hymn was sung only by the clergy who formed the choir. Thus, music became more elaborate in form and structure. Though this clerical choir and elaborate music gave rise to the modern anthem, the practical effect was the exclusion of the people from participation in the hymns.

The Reformation not only recovered many practices of the New Testament and the early church, but it also gave the congregational hymn back to the people. One of the "morning stars" of the Reformation, John Huss of Bohemia, made the beginning. The Hussites, a singing people, were responsible for publishing the first Protestant hymnbook in Prague in 1501.

Perhaps Luther, more than any one other major reformer, stimulated congregational singing. He wrote more than thirty hymns, and some sixty hymnbooks were published during his lifetime. Luther was a somewhat hesitant reformer and wanted to retain the anthems and the chants. However, his followers moved ahead of their leader, and the Lutherans became a great singing people. The Genevan Psalter was published in 1552, and the singing of metric psalms became the usual practice of the reformed churches in Europe and later in America.

Congregational singing as it is known today did not develop until the eighteenth century. The hymns of Isaac Watts and John and Charles Wesley gave rise to this movement. The Wesleyan revival in England, the Great Awakening in America, the later evangelical revival in America, and the frontier revivals—all resulted in a tradition of congregations singing hymns and gospel songs. This practice developed a vast storehouse of evangelical music. Some believe that the Reformation reached its highest point of success when the New Testament pattern of congregational singing was so nearly restored.[1]

II. A Variety of Praise

From this heritage of musical praise, many different types of praise have come into being. A knowledge of these types, both vocal and instrumental, will help worship leaders to give variety to praise in a given service.

1. *Prelude*

The prelude is primarily an aid to worship. It calls attention to the fact that public worship is beginning, and it creates an atmosphere where true worship is possible. The prelude creates an attitude of expectancy in the worshiper as the beginning of the service approaches.

2. *Choral Call to Worship*

A call to worship reminds the worshiper that worship is beginning. Its first aim is to center attention upon God. A call to worship may be spoken or sung. A choral call to worship, such as "The Lord Is in His Holy Temple," not only calls the people to worship, but also is an act of praise itself.

3. *Responses*

Another kind of praise is the response. This is usually a response to prayer and may be a prayer continued. Though the response may serve as an aid to worship, it may also be an act of worship. In the New Testament, the people responded with the "Amen!" A choral amen is for the people. "Hear Our Prayer, O Lord" may express the heart's desire of the congregation. Congregations could sing such responses.

4. *Solo and Ensemble Music*

Another kind of praise is the solo and ensemble music, or "special music." The choir, a small group, or a soloist may contribute the "extra" praise to the service. Such special praise may lift the congregation to an even higher level of worship. Often, the theme of such praise is akin to the theme of the sermon and creates an atmosphere for it. Also, the theme of this special praise may be related to the objective of the message and can open the way for its fulfilment. Care should be taken that the music by the choir or soloist is not performed for its own sake. Musical presentations offered to God and given for his glory stimulate worship.

5. *Hymns*

The hymn is the kind of praise most frequently used. It may be a stately hymn or a gospel song; it may be objective or subjective; it may be addressed to God or to the people. But regardless of type, hymns comprise a large segment of each service. For the congregation to sing with the heart and understanding is in keeping with the spirit of the New Testament. Through the hymns, the congregation may voice its praise to God. This part of the worship belongs to the people and should not be minimized.

III. A VARIETY OF THEMES

Praise is not only of many types, but it also expresses itself in an even greater variety of themes. A casual perusal of the contents of the *Baptist Hymnal*, pages vii-viii, gives these general subject headings:

1. General Worship
2. God the Father
3. Jesus Christ the Son
4. The Holy Spirit
5. The Word of God
6. Salvation
7. The Christian Life
8. The Church
9. The Kingdom of God
10. Missions
11. Social Betterment
12. The Immortal Life

The last two headings list types rather than subjects.

Most of these general headings are further divided. For example, the "Salvation" section has these three divisions:

1. Salvation by Grace
2. Repentance and Confession
3. Invitation and Acceptance

The "Christian Life" section has these subdivisions:

1. Faith and Trust
2. Assurance
3. Hope
4. Love
5. Peace and Comfort
6. Joy
7. Aspiration
8. Prayer
9. Consecration
10. Fellowship
11. The Christian Home

The "Topical Index" lists one hundred and twenty-two topics, or subjects. Almost every important theological and ethical idea is listed. These themes include the major elements of worship—adoration, thanksgiving, confession, petition, and dedication.

IV. CHARACTERISTICS OF PRAISE THROUGH MUSIC

As these praise resources are used, what should characterize the music and hymns selected? What should the worship leader look for in selecting the music?

1. *Theologically Acceptable*

The hymns, anthems, or other music should be in keeping with the theological beliefs of the congregation. They certainly must be in keeping with Christian truth. Some sentimental songs deny the majesty of God. He becomes the "Buddy" or "the Man upstairs" rather than the Lord God, high and lifted up. The "Ave Maria," a prayer to Mary, is used in some evangelical services. But few selections could be more out of harmony with evangelical theology. Praise should be theologically acceptable.

2. *Simplicity in Form and Language*

In choosing hymns, attention should be given to simplicity of form and language. Hymns are not chosen primarily for trained singers. They are chosen for people who generally are not trained musicians. They should have lyric beauty and fine poetic quality, but simplicity in structure is essential if the hymns are to be sung. Hymns that do not meet these requirements will not survive long.

Anthems chosen for the choir may be on a different level of performance. So may the music used for preludes, postludes, and offertories. But that which is chosen for the people and children must be simple.

3. *Singability*

To have a wide use, a hymn must not only be simple, it must also be singable. This is not to say that a tune should be catchy or jazzy, but that it should be singable. The melody should appeal and linger. Since hymns are the means by which the people express praise, the tunes should be those which the people enjoy. Most singable tunes will be those which the people continue to hum or to sing after they have left the worship service.

4. *Fully Understandable*

Hymns or anthems should be understood by the congregation. Most hymns are intelligible, but some solos and anthems are not. These may be sung with great energy and even with great artistic ability, but they mean little to the average congregation if the words are not understood.

Dr. Gaines S. Dobbins has prepared a list of questions which makes an excellent test for hymns and anthems.[2]

Is it singable? Is it within the range of musical ability of choir and congregation?

Is it scriptural? Is the thought in line with and not contrary to the teachings of the Bible?

Has it breadth and depth? Does it reach both Godward and manward, with universal as well as individual appeal?

Is it reverent? Do words and music convey a sense of God's presence and contribute to an attitude of respect?

Is it excellent? Do words and music measure up to a good standard of literary and musical artistry?

Is it useful? Does the song as a whole aid in achieving the planned purpose of the service?

Is it appropriate? Is it suited to the occasion and congruous with other aspects of the service, especially the sermon?

V. FUNCTIONS OF PRAISE

But to what purpose is this praise? What functions are fulfilled by both the vocal and instrumental music?

1. *Congregational Participation*

Hymn singing is an ideal method of congregational participation. By singing the hymns, every worshiper may give expression to every facet of worship. He may praise God, he may give thanks to God, he may confess his sin, he may dedicate himself, or he may show concern for others.

The worshiper may also participate in worship through the anthems and responses. He may make these expressions of praise his own. Ideally this is true. There is no better way for the worshiper to participate in worship than by singing. Here he can fulfil his responsibility of worshiping his God personally.

2. *Creating Oneness*

Praise helps form the individual worshipers into a congregation. Through the prelude, the call to worship, and especially the congregational singing, a sense of oneness is created. A great anthem may give the congregation a sense of being as one before God, certainly one in expression. The minds and hearts of the people are united.

3. *Arousing and Expressing Emotions*

Praise in worship also may cause emotions to be aroused and expressed. The different forms of praise satisfy different emotional needs. A quiet prelude may give a warm feeling of inner peace. A great anthem of praise may arouse a sense of exaltation and joy. A hymn on dedication or surrender may bring deep feelings of guilt and result in confession. But the forms of praise also may be emotional outlets. The worship of God may become so intense that there is need for expression. The hymn is the ideal place for the worshiper to express his emotion. He may sing and shout his joy or happiness. Who has not burst into song when he felt great joy in his heart? To think on God is to praise him.

4. *Instilling Doctrine*

One of the primary functions of praise is education. As a hymn, anthem, or gospel song is sung, ideas expressed by the words are impressed upon the minds. To keep singing an idea may be to accept it. Illion T. Jones insists: "Hymn singing is a method of etching the gospel on the minds and hearts of the worshipers. It is therefore one of the important mediums for transmission of evangelical faith." [3]

VI. ADVICE ABOUT PRAISE THROUGH MUSIC

Since music in worship is important and since many different leaders choose music for many different services, some general counsels about praise may be offered.

1. *Study the Hymnal*

Firsthand knowledge of the hymnal will be of great value to anyone who is responsible for planning worship and selecting hymns. Far too many congregations, departments, unions, circles, and other groups use only a limited number of hymns. The limit is not only in number, but also in the range of themes. A person who has a regular task of selecting hymns should know the contents of the book or books. Most hymnals, including the *Baptist Hymnal,* have a wide variety of hymns. They differ in kind and content. It is the selector's task to know this variety. Have you ever studied the hymnal? Why not? A knowledge of its contents will increase any worship leader's ability to help others in their worship of God.

2. *Select Hymns Which Center in God*

Choose hymns which center in God—God, the Father; God, the Son; and God, the Holy Spirit. Select hymns which praise God for what he has done for man in Christ. Sing hymns which reveal God at work in his mighty redemptive mission. Some songs detract from a God-centered emphasis when they are addreessed to man and not to God. It may not be fitting to eliminate all subjective songs addressed to man, but their use should be limited. Man's praise should be addressed primarily to God.

3. *Select Hymns to Meet Various Needs*

Select hymns to meet the needs of various segments of the congregation. The average congregation has people of various educational, cultural, and age levels. Hymns around a topic or theme may be used, but a varied selection will probably contribute more to the people.

One hymn or one special song may be the only part of the service which has meaning for a worshiper. Therefore, hymns chosen on different, yet related, topics may prove the most helpful to the majority of listeners.

4. *Educate the Congregation in the Great Hymns*

The worship leader or leaders should seek to educate the congregation in the great hymns of the church. Some congregations have not been taught the lofty worship hymns. Some have not been taught a variety of hymns. It is a leader's responsibility to have the best hymnal available and then to teach the people the finest hymns in the book. Southern Baptists now have a comprehensive program of instruction designed to make the best hymns and choral music familiar to each member of the congregation.

5. *Participate in the Praise*

Since congregational singing is one of the few places where each member of the congregation may participate, it must not be bypassed. Yet 50 per cent participation is average fo many congregations. To fail to participate is to fail to worship "Let the people praise thee, O God; let all the people prais thee."

NOTES

[1] Illion T. Jones, *A Historical Approach to Evangelical Worship* (Nashville: Abingdon Press, 1954), p. 258.
[2] *The Church at Worship* (Nashville: Broadman Press, 1962), p. 76.
[3] Jones, *op. cit.*, p. 258.

QUESTIONS TO STIMULATE DISCUSSION

1. Do you like gospel songs? Are they related to the "spiritual songs" that Paul mentions?
2. How many hymns do you know by memory? Have you ever studied the *Baptist Hymnal?* Why not?
3. Do you agree with the theology of the hymns you sing?
4. What characteristics should make hymns suitable for use in worship services?

CHAPTER 7 OUTLINE

I. PRIVATE WORSHIP
   1. The Place
   2. The Time
   3. The Posture
   4. The Worship

II. FAMILY WORSHIP
   1. The Complex Problem
   2. The Ideal Situation
   3. The Present Opportunities
   4. A Catching Faith

III. GROUP WORSHIP

7

Private and Family Worship

IT IS IMPORTANT now to consider private and family worship. Both complete public worship, and both are important to the achievement of real spiritual maturity.

I. PRIVATE WORSHIP

Private worship is essential to a maturing spiritual life. The Christian is often exhorted to engage in private worship or devotion, but is rarely given specific directions of help. What is involved in meaningful private worship? It is doubtful if one Christian can suggest satisfactory plans for another, for private worship is an intensely personal affair. To suggest techniques may be to overemphasize the outward expression of spiritual experiences. Yet those who have regular private devotions follow practices that may be of help to others.

1. *The Place*

A definite place is helpful to one who worships privately. Familiar surroundings may mean that there will be fewer distractions and that a mood of worship may be induced more easily. The choice of a place is usually determined by the worshiper's home, his work, and his community. The corner of a bedroom may be reserved as a place to meet God. An easy chair in the living room or den may be the place. Bibles and devotional aids may be kept on a table nearby to serve both as aids and reminders of worship.

Some Christians go by churches or chapels enroute to

work and use these as places for private worship. Some people have chapels or prayer rooms in the buildings where they work, and they take worship breaks rather than coffee breaks. After other members of the family leave for school or work, many housewives use the kitchen as a place of worship as well as work. On certain days, the place of worship may be the sink, the stove, or the washer. Some Christians engage in private worship as they commute to work by train, bus, subway, or trolley. Some people have outdoor chapels— a secluded spot in the yard, a place in a nearby park, or a favorite spot in the fields. But regardless of the place, a definite place is advantageous for private worship.

2. *The Time*

A regular time for private worship is also essential. This does not mean that one cannot "pray without ceasing" or live in a spirit of communion with God. But spiritual counselors insist that a period of regular, unhurried fellowship with God is basic for spiritual development.

The selection of this time must be left to the individual, for he alone knows his circumstances. For some people, a few minutes in the early morning seem to be the best time. Irregular patterns of work and changing school schedules may make the early morning an extremely hectic time for many adults and their children. Consequently, more Christians are using an evening hour or bedtime as a time for private devotions.

The average person has no control over the time he must go to work or to school, but he can determine the time when he goes to bed. He has more free time then than at any other time during the day. While the morning period has the advantage of beginning the day with God, the evening period allows the believer to review the day and to thank God for his leadership and blessing. Whichever time is chosen as the unhurried period of worship, each day should begin and end with God.

Some people may find time in the midst of the work day for private worship. The particular time selected is not nearly so important as that the time be free from interruptions.

3. *The Posture*

How should one worship? Should he kneel, sit, or stand?

One answer will not suffice for every person. The principle is to worship in the position which is best for him. He may assume the position in which he is most comfortable and that is the most conducive to reverence and receptivity. Some Christians like to kneel when they read the Bible and pray. Others like to sit quietly. Still others prefer to lie quietly as they read and pray. A few worshipers prefer to stand as they would do in public worship. The posture that eliminates the most distractions and makes the worship time the most meaningful should be taken.

4. *The Worship*

What shall be done during the period of private worship? What order should be followed, and what materials should be used? Again, the key words should be freedom and flexibility. Persons follow different patterns, and each person may vary the plan followed from day to day. However, certain acts and materials of worship are common to those who worship privately.

Having assumed the position where it is easiest to turn one's thoughts to God, the worshiper may sing a stanza of a familiar hymn or read a call to worship. Most Christians begin by reading the Bible or some devotional material. Some read a daily devotional guide such as *Open Windows* and then read the Bible. They may read the passage suggested for the day in *The Bible Reader's Guide and Missionary*

Prayer Calendar or the current Training Union quarterly.

Many more people are reading the Bible and discovering its teaching. They may use commentaries or other helps to aid in understanding the message of the Scriptures. The reading of the Bible is usually followed by meditation. What has God said in his Word? How does this apply to the believer's life today? This period of meditation between the reading and prayer can be very meaningful.

Finally comes a time for prayer. This should be the high point of private devotion. One may follow the elements of prayer discussed in chapter 5—adoration, thanksgiving, petition, intercession, confession, and commitment. Usually the believer will let the Spirit of God lead. However, it will prove beneficial to let these elements be present.

Private prayer is one of the best times for one's adoration of God. The worshiper may express love and devotion to his God in a way he would not want to do in public. There are always those persons and things for which the believer will want to express gratitude. Thanks for the grace of God, for the redemptive acts of God in Christ, should never be omitted. Petitions for personal and family needs are always before the worshiper. There will also be many reasons for intercession—for a task in the church, for a lost friend, for a Christian in need, for the world mission of the church, or for an urgent community issue. The Scripture reading will often lead to confession of sin and to new commitment.

Private prayer is individual and personal. One worshiper can hardly direct another. Yet, practices of mature Christians may help others. Regular private worship is one of the essential keys to unlock the way to spiritual maturity.

II. FAMILY WORSHIP

Family worship also has long been a significant part of Christian devotion. Every family that shares in regular family worship will attest to its spiritual contributions. However, no facet of Christian worship has been more affected by a rapidly changing and highly mobile society than has family worship.

1. *The Complex Problem*

In the not too distant past, the family exercised a large measure of control over its time. Often, the parents were at home, or knew precisely when they would leave and return to the home. The children went to school and returned at the same time.

The family pattern is rarely this regular. Competition often determines work hours for the man who is self-employed. The father's work may demand travel, often on short notice. Many men work in plants that operate on swing shifts, and others may be called to work early or be asked to work over-time. Further complications arise when both parents work, often on different schedules. Children may be in different schools and on different schedules. Often the parent at home operates the family "taxi" service for the other members. Little time is left to plan for worship or for other family essentials.

Family worship as it was once known has almost disappeared from many Christian homes. Thus, the question may be asked, What are the opportunities for family worship and what are the plans which are workable today?

2. *The Ideal Situation*

The ideal situation for family worship still is for the entire family to be together at the same time in familiar surroundings that are conducive to a spirit of reverence.

This is the pattern of another generation. Usually, the family gathered in the living room, perhaps before the fireplace. They probably sang hymns, and the father or mother read the Bible. Comments or questions would be offered. Requests for prayer were usually made, and then came prayer time. This family worship service lasted about thirty minutes.

Some families today maintain a similar pattern of family worship. The families who regularly engage in this kind of worship find that it contributes both to spiritual maturity and to family solidarity. For those families who can be together, this plan for family worship remains the ideal.

3. *The Present Opportunities*

But what about the families which do not have the situation where the entire family can be together in the home at a regular time? What opportunities of family worship are open to them?

(1) *Grace at meals.*—The most convenient, yet most meaningful, time of worship may be grace before meals. There will be at least one or two meals when the family will be together. The eating of food not only satisfies a physical need, but it also gives a sense of fellowship and belonging. The meal becomes a spiritual act when God is recognized and his blessing sought.

Most Christian families say grace, return thanks, or ask the blessing. Although the father and mother may pray, the children can share in saying grace. Many Christians will recall this as the first grace they learned to say or sing:

> God is great and God is good;
> We will thank Him for this food;
> By His hand we all are fed;
> Give us, Lord, our daily bread.
>   Amen.

Saying the blessing should not become mere routine. Though the prayer may be brief, it should be said quietly and reverently with a real sense of recognizing the gifts of God. The resurrected Christ was recognized by two of his disciples, not as he talked with them on the road to Emmaus, but as he paused for an ordinary meal with them. As he blessed and broke the bread and shared with them, they knew him. It should be the hope of every Christian family that the presence of Christ will become a reality at each meal. Christ is always present, but sometimes he is not seen. In the act of giving thanks for God's bounty, and in Christ's name, his presence becomes a spiritual reality.

Some families preceded the saying of grace at one meal by Bible reading and prayer. Other families have Bible reading and prayer after one meal. The giving of thanks is actually a part of a larger prayer. Not only is gratitude expressed, but often petitions and intercessions are made for those within and outside of the family. Many Baptist families use their prayer time as an occasion for remembering missionaries. On their birthdays, their names are listed in *Open Windows, The Bible Reader's Guide and Missionary Prayer Calendar*, and the Training Union Bible Readers' Course.

Since the time of grace is often the only time for family worship, this last vestige of family worship should be zealously maintained.

(2) *Once each week.*—Some families who live on an irregular schedule try to set a time for worship each week when all members of the family can be present. A time for the worship is set, and each member of the family reserves this time. At this time, the needs and problems of the family are shared, the Bible is read, and prayer is offered. While this pattern is a poor substitute for daily worship, it does bring the members of the family together once each week. This is far better than a complete neglect of family worship.

(3) *Significant events.*—Some families use the big events as occasions for worship. The new home is offered to God in a dedication service. The birth of a child calls forth praise and thanksgiving to God. The marriage of one of the children reminds the family of God's mercy and providence. Birthdays are generally occasions of gratitude to God for his blessing. Homeleaving and homecoming are times to petition and to thank God. The new job, the enlarged opportunity, the unexpected success provide the renewed desire to turn to

God. For the Christian, faith is not separated from ordinary life. In routine living, God becomes more real.

(4) *Family crises.*—Family crises drive families to worship. Financial difficulty, unexpected illness, and tragic death shake people out of a false sense of independence and cause them to seek their God. In crises, families discuss spiritual and eternal concerns. A house becomes again a house of prayer. Out of the crises comes a new faith in God.

(5) *Decision times.*—Some families turn to God in times of decision. The alternatives are placed before God, and his guidance is sought. Should the new position be accepted? Should the house in the country be bought? Which college should the son or daughter attend? What is the best plan of saving? These and other decisions cause families to seek God.

(6) *Sunday worship together.*—Some families always try to share in public worship. This may be the only time of worship together, or it may be in addition to many other occasions of family worship. But the family feels a sense of oneness and belonging as it shares in common worship. In some Baptist churches, even to worship together is difficult because each member of the family attends a different class or union in a different building. However, when it can be done, worship together is helpful.

4. *A Catching Faith*

A constant Christian atmosphere in the home may be more important than set times of worship. It is possible to have the kind of family life where the Christian faith is more caught than taught. Christian attitudes and principles are constantly in the background and pervade all the activities.

In such a family, belief in God is assumed, not argued. Reverence for God is not proclaimed, but practiced. Public worship is a natural part of family life. Family problems are settled in the light of Christian teaching. The highest ideals are taught; great expectations are assumed. The children who grow and develop in this home are most fortunate, indeed.

It is not easy to let the Christian faith simply pervade family life. To discuss family affairs in the light of Christian teaching may be difficult. Some Christian parents find themselves almost without words when they begin to talk of the things of God. The parent must learn to talk of his faith. In order to do this, Christian parents must keep their faith uppermost in their own minds. They must reach definite conclusions themselves. When one father and mother were asked what ideals they were teaching their children, they could only mutter, "We want them to be good."

III. GROUP WORSHIP

Small, intimate group worship is similar in nature to private and family worship. Some use this kind of worship to enlarge private and family worship. Some businessmen have times of study and worship. Increasingly, Christian men use the breakfast or lunch period for group worship. Groups of women meet to listen to records of sermons or Bible expositions. Small groups of students meet in high schools and colleges for worship. Many college students will recall the helpfulness of morning watch or evening prayer.

Some young people, away from the family for the first time, find that group worship is a good substitute for family worship. Roommates become worship partners.

If the worshiper has tried periods of private, family, and group worship repeatedly and has not been able to sustain these periods, he should not despair. Each meaningful effort will make the next more meaningful.

QUESTIONS TO STIMULATE DISCUSSION

1. Do you engage in planned private worship?
2. Do you have periods of family worship?
3. What problems do you have in private and family worship?
4. What worship experience is most meaningful to you? Why?

CHAPTER 8 OUTLINE

8

Worship in Life

CONGREGATIONS ARE OFTEN URGED to beware of idol worship. Those parts of Christendom that have images in their sanctuaries may be tempted to engage in actual idol worship. However, the danger confronting the average Christian is not the worship of graven images. It is the creation of idols out of things and then the worship of the things. There is always the temptation to worship the things which God has given, rather than the God who gave them. This transfer of allegiance may be quite unconscious, but it happens very easily.

There may be an even more subtle temptation confronting the regular worshiper. Rather than falling into *idol* worship, the average Christian may engage in *idle* worship. He may attend services and share in the order of worship, but the worship is idle. It has no continuing or vital relationship to the life he lives.

I. WORSHIP WITHOUT FOLLOW-THROUGH

There is increasing evidence in Southern Baptist life that worship does not always result in positive Christian living or service. While Southern Baptists now claim to be the largest evangelical denomination in the United States, recent studies reveal these facts about its more than 10,000,000 members. Approximately 50 per cent are inactive. These people are nonresident or almost totally unenlisted church members. Less than 50 per cent of the total membership is enrolled in Sunday school, and only 55 per cent of those enrolled are present on a given Sunday. This means that only 1 out of 4 engages in Bible study on a given Sunday. Less than 25 per cent of the total membership is enrolled in Training Union, and only 55 per cent of those are present on a given Sunday. This means that only about 1 out of 8 shares in a training program Sunday by Sunday.

It is likely that those members sharing in Sunday morning worship would be comparable to those in Sunday school—1 out of 4, and those participating in the evening worship would approximate those in Training Union—1 out of 8. It is highly unlikely that those sharing in the prayer service would be more than 6 per cent of the total membership, or about 1 out of 15. Moreover, only 1 member out of 6 is a tither. In most congregations, 20 per cent of the members provide 80 per cent of the financial support. Only about 1 out of 5 really cares enough to undergird the total program of the church. Even more distressing is the fact that it takes 29 members to reach 1 lost person. The annual ratio of members to baptisms is 29 to 1. This implies that Christ does not mean enough to most members for them to share him with others. While statistics do not tell the whole story, they reveal clearly that there is a discrepancy between profession and practice, between worship and the bearing of spiritual fruit in life.

This statistical story, as bad as it is, does not tell the even more appalling story of low moral standards and the loss of positive spiritual influence. If there was ever a sharp line of demarcation between those in the church and those outside the church, that line no longer exists. The high divorce rate, the increase in alcoholism, sexual promiscuity, illegitimacy, petty theft, dishonesty—these and other evils have not only pervaded society but are also found in the church. Whereas the church should be good leaven, constantly raising the moral level of society, just the opposite seems to be true. Many present-day Christians are in the world and of the world. The world points an accusing finger at the church and says, "You are like us." It is quite ironical that in a day when more people are going to church than ever before, the positive influence is less than ever before.

II. THE FRUITS OF WORSHIP

Real Christian worship should affect the lives of all who participate in it. Whenever man truly worships his God—whether in private, family, or corporate worship—there is a new sense of commitment. When he has fellowship with God, man wants to be with God and to do for God. Many new spiritual impulses stir in the worshiper's heart.

1. *A Sense of God*

Every encounter with God gives the worshiper a new and heightened sense of God. Having personally communed with God, the sense of God remains. The believer becomes God intoxicated. The God of Sunday and of the Sunday worship hours becomes the God of other days and other hours. The believer can truly say that in God he lives and moves and has his being. The affairs of the home, the job, the school, and the party are performed within a consciousness that God is sharing. Daily life becomes a great adventure that is shared with, and is under the dominion of, the triune God. Truly, the believer lives under the shadow of the Almighty.

2. *"Instant" Worship*

From a sense of God comes what may be called "instant" worship. Because the believer is in fellowship with God, many are the unplanned times during the day when he worships God. In the glory of a sunrise that announces a new day, the Christian thinks of God. In each opportunity of service, the believer sees the providence of God. In the midst of difficulty and pain, the child of God is conscious of God's undergirding. For the opportunities of each day and for the resources equal to those opportunities, the Christian sees the provision of God's grace.

This instant worship often expresses itself in short, unplanned exclamations of prayer. These may or may not be spoken. But each day brings unexpected blessings of grace and calls for unplanned words of thanks to the ever-present God. Each day brings its unanticipated needs and calls forth its cries of petition. Some days bring moments of unguarded temptation and resulting sin. This sudden burden of guilt brings repentance, and a cry of confession is wrung from the believer.

3. *Sharing of Possessions*

From true worship comes a heightened sense of stewardship to God, who has made lavish provision for his children. To worship God, in reality, is to recognize his absolute sovereignty. Man recognizes that he is under God and that he is God's steward, or tenant. Because he and all he has comes from God, the believer wants to render a good stewardship.

One expression of this will be the sharing of possessions with God. The Lord God created all things. What every man has was first God's. In a real sense, man is God's guest. The worshiper wants to share with God. Worship is offering, but worship also stimulates offering. The believer gives his tithes and offering as worship and as a response to worship. The Christian not only brings an offering and comes into God's courts, but because he has been in God's courts, he wants to bring other offerings.

This is not unusual. Once man knows, loves, and belongs to God, he will not withhold from God. The apostle Paul had great insight when he said to the Corinthians, "I seek not yours, but you" (2 Cor. 12:14). Paul knew that man must first give himself to God. Then having given himself, he will give his possessions cheerfully, even hilariously. In response to the riches of God's grace, the believer sings:

> Were the whole realm of nature mine,
>   That were a present far too small;
> Love so amazing, so divine,
>   Demands my soul, my life, my all.
>
>   —ISAAC WATTS

4. Redeeming the Time

The true worshiper also will offer his time to God. Time is life, and, having worshiped God, the Christian offers his life anew. He is not his own; he is bought with a price. He cannot and will not say, "I can do as I please." His time is God's. He believes the apostolic call to make the most of his time. (See Eph. 5:16.)

The Christian offers his God not only the Sunday hours, but all the hours of the week. Time is to be lived under God and invested for God. How can time best be used? What should have priority? The child of God must do some sorting both between the good and the bad, and between the necessary and the unnecessary. Time must not be wasted, but rather it must be redeemed, bought up.

Every Christian needs to raise this question within himself, What am I doing now that I could stop doing without hurting myself physically or spiritually? Time is life. If life is to be offered to God, then so must the best of one's time. Worship is offering, and time is one of the believer's choice offerings to God.

5. Serving the Lord

A natural response to worship in spirit and in truth is serving God. Because he worships God, the Christian's zeal does not flag. Rather he is "fervent in spirit; serving the Lord" (Rom. 12:11). Isaiah's response was a normal response. He had confronted his God, and now he was ready to serve God.

He responded to God's call, "Here am I; send me" (Isa. 6:8). Jesus asked Simon Peter, "Do you love me?" and Peter responded, "You know that I love you." Then, Jesus said, "Tend my sheep." (See John 21.) Jesus seemed to be saying, "If you love me, serve me and my people." The worshiper does not have to be urged to serve. The desire to serve rises spontaneously within him.

Service to God finds many avenues of expression. In a Baptist church, the opportunities of service are legion. The Sunday school, Training Union, Woman's Missionary Union, and Brotherhood offer many opportunities. Every community provides almost limitless opportunities for service. The people are as sheep without a shepherd. The downtrodden need to be uplifted; the distraught, to be comforted; the sick, a healing hand; the misguided, counsel—the list of needs is almost endless. But one who has been in God's presence will want to minister in God's stead.

6. *The Children of God*

Perhaps the worship of God more than any other factor makes man aware of the oneness of all men. When God, the Father of all men, is worshiped, the worshiper cannot escape the fact that all men have a common heritage.

The Christian, who has the gift of salvation in Christ, knows that Christ died not only for him, but for all men. A great personal worship experience caused Simon Peter to rise above the narrow view that all other men were inferior to the Jews. Peter was compelled to exclaim, "I most certainly understand now that God is not one to show partiality, but in every nation the man who fears Him and does what is right, is welcome to Him" (Acts 10:34–35, NASB). Everyone who is welcome to God as his child should be welcomed by another child of God.

Truly, in Christ all men are made one. They are one with Christ and one with each other because they are in Christ.

God created all men, redeemed all men by Jesus Christ, and dwells in all believers by his Holy Spirit. Thus through the worship of God, there comes to the worshiper a sense of fellowship with all men.

7. Personal Consecration

The worship of God also brings intense self-examination and a deepened sense of personal consecration. To worship a holy God is to become acutely aware of one's own unholiness. Isaiah's experience is the norm for all who worship God in spirit and in truth. When he saw the "Lord sitting upon a throne, high and lifted up" (Isa. 6:1), he truly saw himself. Consternation filled his heart and confession leaped to his lips: "Woe is me! for I am undone; because I am a man of unclean lips, and I dwell in the midst of a people of unclean lips: for mine eyes have seen the King, the Lord of hosts" (Isa. 6:5).

To be in God's presence always brings a new desire for personal holiness and righteousness. Worship brings repentance, confession, and a new commitment. Worship causes the believer to want to fulfil Peter's exhortation: "But like the Holy One who called you, be holy yourselves also in all your behavior; because it is written, 'You shall be holy, for I am holy'" (1 Peter 1:15, NASB).

For the Christian "to walk in a manner worthy of the calling" (Eph. 4:1, NASB) to which he has been called is never easy. His human weakness and natural inclination to sin makes it almost impossible to achieve. His one hope is in the regular, constant worship of his holy God. Most pastors notice that those who worship Sunday by Sunday rarely dishonor their Lord and their church by their behavior. Pastors also observe that the members who no longer worship drift easily into worldly temptations and the snare of the devil. Worship provides a great corrective and a great spiritual strength. Worship keeps the goal of holiness before the believer. Moreover, the inner power to make the goal a reality also comes to him in worship.

8. Inspires Witness

True worship always inspires witness. To worship God is to remember his redemptive acts in man's behalf. For the believer to recall the riches of God's grace so freely offered to all men in Christ is to have kindled within him a desire to tell other men this good news.

Contrary to opinions, there is no conflict between worship and witness. One writer may claim that worship is the primary function of the church; another may insist that witness is the first duty of the church. Actually, each is primary in its own realm. Worship is the church's first responsibility to itself. The church cannot live without worship. On the other hand, witness is the church's first responsibility to the world. The church cannot live without witness. Worship and witness are not in conflict. They are the twin duties of the church. When seen in proper perspective, each is primary in its own realm. Worship should recreate a desire to witness. Witness should send the child of God back to worship.

In what ways will worship inspire witness? When the child of God turns from his sin and reconsecrates himself, a new desire to witness comes to him. David cried to God and prayed for forgiveness of sin, "Hide thy face from my sins, and blot out all mine iniquities" (Psalm 51:9). Then, he could promise God, "Then will I teach transgressors thy ways: and sinners shall be converted unto thee" (Psalm 51:13). When cleansed of sin, the believer has a renewed desire to witness.

Worship also gives motivation for witness. The command "You shall be My witness" (Acts 1:8, NASB) is often heard with almost total indifference. The importance of the command is accepted, but there is no inner compulsion to fulfil it. Here, worship does its essential work. As joy fills the worshiper's heart, and the peace that passes understanding pervades his being, there is an inner compulsion to share the riches of God's grace with others.

Worship also reminds the witness of his message. As he hears the proclamation of the good news, he remembers the glorious story of the reconciliation God has brought in Christ. As he sings the old, old story, it is wonderfully sweet and worth telling. As the witness prays in Jesus' name, he knows anew that eternal life is through his Lord's name.

Thus, worship and witness are part of each other. They are bound together, and worship contributes to witness.

9. Living Hope

Worship keeps the believer's eternal hope real and vital. The Christian has fully accepted the promises of Jesus Christ. He has heard Jesus say, "I am the resurrection, and the life; he who believes in Me shall live even if he dies, and everyone who lives and believes in Me shall never die" (John 11:25-26, NASB). Jesus also promised. "I go to prepare a place for you. And if I go and prepare a place for you, I will come again, and receive you unto myself; that where I am, there ye may be also" (John 14:2-3). Jesus also declared, "I give unto them eternal life; and they shall never perish, neither shall any man pluck them out of my hand" (John 10:28). The Holy Spirit seals these promises in the heart of every believer. Then, as the Christian worships the living God, a living hope burns within him. The worship of God brings a new certainty of life everlasting.

Worship unrelated to life is not true worship and is not pleasing to God. Genuine worship should affect every facet of the worshiper's life. Worship should bring all of his life under God's dominion. When the life of the worshiper is not changed, when his horizons are not lifted, when his resources are not increased, then God has not been worshiped in truth and in spirit. For to worship truly is to share power from the omnipotent (all-powerful) God and to receive wisdom from the omniscient (all-knowing) God. Real worship draws man nearer to the God he worships. True worship causes the image of God to be seen more clearly in the worshiper. "O come, let us worship and bow down: let us kneel before the Lord our maker. For he is our God" (Psalm 95:6-7).

QUESTIONS TO STIMULATE DISCUSSION

1. Does the church exert positive Christian influences in your community?
2. What is meant by "idle" worship?
3. How does one's worship affect his life?
4. How does one's worship affect his outlook and attitudes?

For Review and Written Work

CHAPTER 1

1. What percentage of the Christians in your city worship each Sunday? Give an estimate.
2. Does your congregation "worship" the pastor?
3. Is worship important? List five reasons.
4. How can one develop a desire for more meaningful worship experiences?

CHAPTER 2

5. What is the derivation of our word "worship"?
6. What is your own definition of worship?
7. List the qualities which characterized New Testament worship.
8. Should worship be free or formal? Explain.

CHAPTER 3

9. What are some biblical examples related to present-day worship?
10. List five moods of worship.
11. What qualities characterize good worship planning?
12. Why is participation in worship important?

CHAPTER 4

13. What is the place of the Bible in worship? in public worship? in private worship?
14. Should a sermon have a text? Is the Bible important to preaching?
15. Is the sermon an act of worship? If so, why? If not, why not?
16. How may the congregation help the pastor preach more effectively?

CHAPTER 5

17. List the basic elements of prayer.
18. In what different ways may corporate, or public, prayer be expressed?
19. Who should lead public prayer?
20. List the qualities that should characterize public prayer.

CHAPTER 6

21. What was the first hymnbook used by Christians?
22. How many general subject headings are listed in the contents of the *Baptist Hymnal*? List some of them.
23. How does the singing of hymns help one to worship?
24. How does the singing of hymns instil doctrine?

CHAPTER 7

25. What is your pattern of private worship?
26. Do you say grace before each meal?
27. Have you participated in small group worship other than family worship? What group or groups?

CHAPTER 8

28. Should worship be related to life? If so, why?
29. What did the author mean by "instant" worship?
30. Has your worship brought you to new levels of personal commitment? Explain.

A Selected Bibliography

THE FOLLOWING BOOKS offer further study in the subject matter of each chapter. The student will want to develop his knowledge of some areas of worship pertinent to his work and interest.

CHAPTER 1

BOWMAN, CLARICE. *Restoring Worship.* New York: Abingdon-Cokesbury Press, 1951.

DOBBINS, GAINES S. *The Church at Worship.* Nashville: Broadman Press, 1962.

DOUGLASS, TRUMAN B. *Why Go to Church?* New York: Harper & Bros., 1957.

PALMER, ALBERT W. *The Art of Conducting Public Worship.* New York: Macmillan Co., 1939.

CHAPTER 2

ABBA, RAYMOND. *Principles of Christian Worship.* New York: Oxford University Press, 1957.

DAVIS, H. GRADY. *Why We Worship.* Philadelphia: Fortress Press, 1961.

HORTON, DOUGLASS. *The Meaning of Worship.* New York: Harper & Bros., 1959.

CHAPTER 3

DAVIES, HORTON. *Christian Worship.* New York: Abingdon Press, 1957.

DOBBINS, GAINES S. *The Church at Worship.* Nashville: Broadman Press, 1962.

HERBERT, A. S. *Worship in Ancient Israel.* Richmond: John Knox Press, 1959.

JONES, ILLION T. *A Historical Approach to Evangelical Worship.* New York: Abingdon Press, 1954. Chapter 12.

MOULE, C. F. D. *Worship in the New Testament.* Richmond: John Knox Press, 1962.

CHAPTER 4

ALLMEN, JEAN JACQUES VON. *Preaching and the Congregation.* Richmond: John Knox Press, 1962.

BROWNE, R. E. C. *The Ministry of the Word.* Naperville: Alex R. Allenson, Inc., 1958.

CAIRNS, FRANK. *The Prophet of the Heart*. New York: Harpers & Bros., 1935. Pages 27–63.

FORSYTH, P. T. *Positive Preaching and Modern Mind*. Naperville: Alex R. Allenson, Inc., 1953. Pages 75–110.

KEIR, THOMAS H. *The Word in Worship*. New York: Oxford University Press, 1962.

NOYES, M. P. *Preaching the Word of God*. New York: Charles Scribner's Sons, 1943. Pages 173–208.

PEARSON, ROY. *The Preacher: His Purpose and Practice*. Philadelphia: The Westminster Press, 1963. Pages 125–40.

SANGSTER, W. E. *An Approach to Preaching*. Philadelphia: The Westminster Press, 1952.

WINGREN, GUSTAF. *The Living Word*. Philadelphia: Fortress Press, 1960.

CHAPTER 5

BLACKWOOD, ANDREW J. *Leading in Public Prayer*. Nashville: Abingdon Press, 1958.

BUTTRICK, GEORGE A. *Prayer*. Nashville: Abingdon Press, 1942.

FOX, S. F. *A Chain of Prayer Across the Ages*. New York: E. P. Dutton & Co., 1930.

GARRETT, CONSTANCE. *Growth in Prayer*. New York: Macmillan Co., 1953.

HARKNESS, GEORGIA. *Prayer and the Common Life*. Nashville: Abingdon Press, 1948.

NOYES, MORGAN PHELPS. *Prayers for Services*. New York: Charles Scribner's Sons, 1934.

WILLIAMSON, ROBERT L. *Effective Public Prayer*. Nashville: Broadman Press, 1960.

CHAPTER 6

ASHTON, J. N. *Music in Worship*. Philadelphia: United Church Press, 1943.

COFFIN, H. S. *The Public Worship of God*. Philadelphia: Westminster Press, 1946.

HOOPER, WILLIAM LOYD. *Church Music in Transition*. Nashville: Broadman Press, 1963.

LOVELACE, AUSTIN C. and RICE, WILLIAM C. *Music and Worship in the Church*. Nashville: Abingdon Press, 1960.

MAXWELL, WILLIAM D. *An Outline of Christian Worship*. London: Oxford University Press, 1936.

REYNOLDS, WILLIAM J. *Hymns of Our Faith*. Nashville: Broadman Press, 1964.

——, A *Survey of Christian Hymnody*. New York: Holt, Rinehart and Winston, Inc., 1963.

ROUTLEY, ERIC. *Church Music and Theology*. Philadelphia: Fortress Press, 1960.

SYDNOR, JAMES R. *The Hymn and Congregational Singing*. Richmond: John Knox Press, 1960.

© THE LOCKMAN FOUNDATION, La Habra, Calif., 1960, 1962, 1963. *New American Standard Bible*, New Testament. Published by Broadman Press, Nashville, Tenn.

CHAPTER 7

ADAMS, THEODORE F. *Making Your Marriage Succeed*. New York: Harper & Bros., 1953.

BOWMAN, CLARICE. *Restoring Worship*. New York: Abingdon-Cokesbury Press, 1951.

HARKNESS, GEORGIA. *Prayer and the Common Life*. New York: Abingdon-Cokesbury Press, 1948.

TRUEBLOOD, ELTON and PAULINE. *The Recovery of Family Life*. New York: Harper & Bros., 1953.

CHAPTER 8

BOWMAN, CLARICE. *Restoring Worship*. New York: Abingdon-Cokesbury Press, 1951.

HAHN, WILHELM. *Worship and Congregation*. Richmond: John Knox Press, 1963.

McKAY, ARTHUR R. *Servants and Stewards*. Philadelphia: Westminster Press, 1963.

Teaching Helps

J. Henry Coffer, Jr.

PREPARATION

Secure the following materials for use during the week or sessions of study:

1. Four copies of your church bulletin
2. One copy of your church hymnal for each member of the class
3. Several issues of *Home Life*
4. Several issues of *The Secret Place,* if they are available
5. Several issues of *The Upper Room,* if they are available
6. Several issues of *Open Windows*
7. Several issues of *The Bible Reader's Guide and Missionary Prayer Calendar*
8. Several issues of the current Training Union quarterlies for Adults

Secure and display the books listed at the end of each chapter of the book. Ask your church librarian to purchase some of these books for use during and after the study.

Ask the members of your class to bring their Bibles to each session. Plan to use them.

Ask one member of the class to serve as "secretary" to keep notes of suggestions which come out of the group discussions. Review these suggestions at the end of the week for practical approaches to the appreciation and improvement of worship in your church.

CHAPTER 1

Begin your first session with these questions: What do you think of worship? What do you get out of it? Write the replies at the top of the chalkboard. Introduce the book by showing that it deals with these questions in some depth. Review the chapter headings with the class and indicate the amount of time you will be spending on each chapter.

Spend the major portion of the hour on section I. Ask the class to rephrase in their own words each of the ten reasons given for the importance of worship. List these on the chalkboard.

They are:

1. To sustain a sense of Oneness with God
2. To fulfil Our Need for Fellowship
3. To give purpose and meaning to life
4. To make us aware of our limitations
5. To find answers to life's problems
6. To gain strength to live abundantly
7. To change perspective
8. To receive instruction
9. To renew a desire for service
10. To receive salvation and assurance

Give out copies of your church bulletin and ask: how does our church worship service meet these needs? If there are any needs omitted, how can the service be improved so as to include them?

Review briefly the examples in section II. Reread the replies at the top of the chalkboard. Are there any evidences of a depreciation of worship? Ask the class to share personal experiences of such.

Conclude with a brief review of section III. Introduce the class to the books on your display table and/or those available in your church library.

CHAPTER 2

Review quickly the introductory paragraphs. Then divide the class into four groups. Ask each group to read and discuss one of the approaches to a definition of worship found in section I. After a few minutes, reassemble the class and ask a spokesman from each group to report. In the light of this discussion, ask the class to develop its own definition.

Give out copies of your church bulletin and, using it to illustrate your points, review the eight characteristics of Christian worship in section II. Ask the four groups to reassemble and assign to each group the following task: Plan a service of worship in which these characteristics are consciously included. After several minutes bring the groups together to share the fruits of their work. What are some of the changes from your present service? Discuss the merits of each.

CHAPTER 3

Briefly review section I. Then give class members something of the flavor and excitement of Jewish worship by engaging in a responsive reading as if they were meeting in the Temple or an early synagogue.

Ask them to turn to Psalm 105. Point out the responsive nature of each verse: the second half of each verse repeats the thought of the first. This parallelism is characteristic of much of Hebrew poetry. The priest would sing or chant the first half of the verse and the people would respond by putting the same thought into their own words—as if to say, "Yes, we are listening, we understand, and we feel the same way."

Read Psalm 105 as follows: you read the first half of each verse. Ask the class to respond with the second half of the verse.

Lecture briefly on worship in the apostolic period. Ask someone to read the quotation from Justin Martyr (in part 2 of Sec. I) and compare the service described with that of your church.

Ask the class to keep their bulletins before them as you discuss the "moods of worship" in section II. Ask them to check those places in the service in which each mood is found; e.g., hymns of *praise*, the prayer of *confession*, etc.

Here is the list from chapter 3:

1. Recognition
2. Praise
3. Confession
4. Illumination
5. Dedication

Continue this "bulletin check" with the "principles of planning" in the same section. Ask the class to note the *order* of your service. What are the strengths and weaknesses of your present "order of worship"? How long has it been since there have been any changes in it?

Discuss briefly the suggestions offered in section III.

These include:
1. Preparation
2. Participation
3. Reverence

Ask: Do we have any problems in these areas on which we need to work? What specifically can we do to improve?

In conclusion, ask the class to look at the architecture and furnishings of your church. What are some of the truths represented by them, for example, by an open Bible on the pulpit? a steeple? the baptistry? the position of the pulpit? the windows? the Lord's Supper table? Are some things represented which are contrary to your beliefs as a church? What are your strongest and most meaningful symbols? One or two members of the class may wish to do a follow-up study on the symbols in your church to share with visitors.

CHAPTER 4

Begin this session by asking the class to examine the approach to Bible reading in your worship services. Are many sections of the Bible read over a period of time or are only a few passages used again and again? Distribute copies of your church hymnal and point out the organization and number of responsive readings. Discuss ways to use such readings to achieve a balanced diet of Scripture reading in your worship.

In discussing the uses of the Bible in worship, ask the class to consider ways of using portions of the following psalms as "calls to worship": 95; 96; 98; 100. Illustrate "offertory sentences" in 2 Corinthians 9:6-8; John 3:16; and Malachi 3:10. Members of the class may wish to memorize the "benedictions" in Numbers 6:24-26; 2 Corinthians 13:14; and Jude 24-25.

As you approach suggestions for Scripture reading, ask three members of the class to read aloud short passages. Two of them will break the rules suggested under this heading. The third will try to read well. Ask the class to decide which readings were most conducive to worship and why.

In approaching section II, ask why a knowledge of the sermon's place in worship is important for the congregation. Present the material on "the sermon as worship" in the form of a friendly debate by three members of the class. Conclude with a review of the remaining parts of this section. Ask: How can we make our people more aware of their part in the preaching services?

Below is listed the subheads listed under section II:

1. The centrality of preaching
2. The nature of the sermon
3. The sermon as worship
4. The sermon and the Supper
5. The congregation's part in the preaching

CHAPTER 5

In discussing the nature of public prayer, distinguish between "public prayer" and the "praying in public" condemned by Jesus in Matthew 6:5-6.

Write the elements of prayer (sec. II) on the chalkboard.

1. Adoration
2. Thanksgiving
3. Confession
4. Petition
5. Intercession
6. Dedication

As you define each element, ask the class to call out phrases to illustrate it from prayers they have heard. Ask the class to compose a brief prayer which will incorporate all of these elements. Direct them to look at your service of worship to see whether there are certain prayers which incorporate one element to a greater extent than others. Can they find all the elements of prayer included in the service?

1. The invocation
2. The pastoral prayer
3. The offertory prayer
4. The prayer after the sermon
5. The benediction

List on the chalkboard the types of prayer described in part 2 of section III.

1. Extemporaneous prayer
2. Planned public prayer
3. The collect
4. The litany
5. Bidding prayer
6. Silent prayer

Read the sample collect, noting the divisions: the "address to deity," the "who clause," the "petition," the "result," and the "ending." Ask each member to compose a collect. Read some of their collects aloud. Then, in a group effort, compose a "bidding" prayer.

Conclude with a brief lecture on section IV. As you review

the "qualities of prayer," ask the class to apply these criteria to the prayers they have just composed.

CHAPTER 6

Present the material in section I in a brief lecture. Then ask a pianist to play a selection from each type of worship music in section II. With hymnals in hand, lead the class in singing a choral call to worship, a prayer response, and one stanza of a hymn.

Now call their attention to the table of contents at the front of the Hymnal and to the topical index at the back. Point out the various indexes in your hymnal and the ways in which each one can be used most effectively in planning for worship.

Outline section IV on the chalkboard as you present it. Point out that the editors of the hymnal considered these characteristics in selecting hymns for inclusion in the hymnal. If a favorite hymn was left out, see whether it failed to measure up to one of these requirements. Here is the outline for section IV:

1. Theologically acceptable
2. Simplicity in form and language
3. Singability
4. Fully understandable

Now turn to section V and discuss it in terms of the characteristics listed on the board. Ask: Which functions are related to which characteristics? Show these relationships on the chalkboard.

Present the material in section VI, concluding with a discussion of the following: What is your reaction to an unfamiliar hymn? How long has it been since you learned a new hymn? How can your church develop or improve its program for the teaching and appreciation of new hymns? How can you help?

CHAPTER 7

Make a display of materials for private and family worship. Ask your class members to bring any helpful materials they may have to share.

Ask the class to supplement the suggestions for private worship in section I with ideas from their own experience.

Present the first two parts of section II briefly. Then spend the major portion of your time on parts 3 and 4. List the opportunities for family worship on the chalkboard and ask the class to share their experiences in these areas. Are there other opportunities which the class can add to the list? Ask especially for examples of ways in which "faith" has been "caught" in their homes.

Stress the positive emphasis in the concluding paragraph: don't despair!

CHAPTER 8

Begin your discussion by having two members of the class read aloud Amos 5:21–24 and Isaiah 1:10–20. Point out that these prophets were speaking out against empty worship, namely, worship without fruits in life (sec. I).

Review the meaning of worship (chap. 2), stressing the notion of a commitment to that which is most "worthy." Discuss the fruits of worship in the light of this commitment to God. How is each fruit related to this central meaning? Write each one of the fruits of worship on the chalkboard and ask the class to give a concrete illustration of each for your church. How does your church measure up? Ask each member of the class to ask this question of himself. Lead in prayer that the results of this study may include a vital renewal on every level of life both as individuals and as a church.